# Straight Arrow:
## The Definitive Radio Log and Resource Guide For That Legendary Indian Figure On the Trail of Justice

## WHAT OTHERS ARE SAYING:

"The sagebrush and juniper covered hills of Eastern Oregon may or may not have been Nabisco's idea of Straight Arrow Country. But to a nine year old cowboy hunkered down in front of the radio, Straight Arrow, Packy and Molly lived through their adventures protecting the innocents on wagon trains and righting the wrongs in the untamed West. I was hooked and collected all the those mysterious premiums and informative Injun Uity cards, which, by the way, I still have.

Years later and long ago I met my friend and fellow collector, Bill Harper. He added several new dimensions to Straight Arrow-knowledge, research, the actors on the radio and a connection for our hobby—Pow Wow, the Straight Arrow newsletter. I have always admired and envied his publishing background, tenacity and uncanny ability to dig out well-hidden tidbits of Straight Arrow Lore. His consummate skills and sincere interest assure a good read and the definitive Straight Arrow."

Gary Fugate – Straight Arrow collector extraordinary,<br>historian and gold miner

"Over the years, the term "straight arrow" has woven its way into the tapestry of American vernacular to identify someone as being clean cut, with moral and spiritual values—beyond all reproach.

And so it was 55 years ago, children of all ages gathered around the family radio and listened to the adventures of a Comanche Indian who upheld these values and fought to keep the west free from law breakers and other devious denizens of degradation. The Lone Ranger, if you remember, rode a great white horse named, Silver, shot bullets of the same ore and had a faithful Indian companion.

Straight Arrow had a white sidekick, shot gold tipped arrows and rode a golden palomino. Both stood for and upheld the same set of values. If the formula worked for the masked man—it certainly proved successful for Straight Arrow.

Bill Harper has delved deep into the interiors of the golden cave, digging and panning for any and all remnants of history concerning this fascinating character—Straight Arrow (both radio and print).

The fruit of his labors are contained in this book and after reading its pages, we are now privileged to wear the two red feathered head band! Kaneewah, Fury!"

Jim Scancarelli – Artist and writer of<br>Gasoline Alley—the comic strip

"Riding out of the past and filling the imaginations of children of the 1950s was just part of what Straight Arrow was. Orphaned at an early age, raised by ranchers, it was not until his adulthood that Straight Arrow discovered that he was a Native American. He then took on the trappings of his Indian heritage, and riding his golden palomino, he brought justice to the world.

The character came alive in comic books, in the daily newspaper, on radio, and even in cereal boxes, where Indian facts and skills were included as inserts for boys and girls to collect. Useful information and uncommon skills were treasured by children, parents and scoutmasters.

No one has researched the heritage of Straight Arrow more thoroughly than Bill Harper. Every nook and cranny that held any information about the character, and the people who played him on the radio, who wrote the scripts, or drew the comics—he has searched it out, and presents with this book the most definitive history of Straight Arrow. Come relive the days of yesteryear in the pages of this book—or discover Straight Arrow for the first time, and you find in him a force for good and a fund of knowledge.

Kanewah, Fury!"

Jean Walton – A collector maintaining a internet site;<br>A Collectible Site for The Shredded Wheat Company

# Straight Arrow:
## The Definitive Radio Log and Resource Guide For That Legendary Indian Figure On the Trail of Justice

by William H. Harper

BearManor Media
2007

Straight Arrow:
The Definitive Radio Log and Resource Guide For That Legendary
Indian Figure On the Trail of Justice

© 2007 William H. Harper

For information, address:

**BearManor Media**
P. O. Box 71426
Albany, GA 31708

bearmanormedia.com

Cover design by John Teehan

Typesetting and layout by John Teehan

Published in the USA by BearManor Media

ISBN—1-59393-065-8

# Dedication
# Teresa V. Harper
# 1953–1997

*and my children who all
learned to sing the Nabisco's jingle
from the opening of the
Straight Arrow radio show;
Alexander, Bleu, Rosa and Kolbe*

# Table of Contents

Acknowledgements ................................................................................. i

Foreward ............................................................................................... v

Introduction ......................................................................................... 1
    Overview ........................................................................................ 2

Straight Arrow Radio .......................................................................... 7
    Sheldon Stark ............................................................................... 11
    Howard Culver ............................................................................. 13
    Fred Howard (Wright) .................................................................. 16
    Gwen Delano ............................................................................... 18
    Frank Bingman ............................................................................ 19
    Milton Charles ............................................................................. 22
    Ted Robertson .............................................................................. 24
    Ray Kemper ................................................................................. 27

Straight Arrow Radio Log .................................................................. 29

Getting It Right ................................................................................ 105

Straight Arrow in Person .................................................................. 109

Premiums and Merchandise and Others ........................................... 115
    Premiums .................................................................................. 115
    Merchandise .............................................................................. 127
    John C. Walworth ...................................................................... 131
    Novel Novelties .......................................................................... 132
    Straight Arrow Board Game ....................................................... 132
    Others ........................................................................................ 135

Print Media .................................................................................. 137
    Injun-Uity ............................................................................. 137
    Straight Arrow Comics ....................................................... 138
    Vincent Sullivan ................................................................. 139
    Gardner Fox ........................................................................ 140
    Fred L. Meagher ................................................................. 141
    Straight Arrow In the Comics .......................................... 144
    Daily Strip .......................................................................... 156
    John Belfi ............................................................................ 159
    Joe Certa ............................................................................. 160
    Miscellaneous .................................................................... 161

Sources ......................................................................................... 163

Addendum .................................................................................. 165

A word about the author ........................................................... 171

# Acknowledgements

It is an awesome process to produce a manuscript and there are many persons to thanks. God should always be foremost but sometimes we forget.

To thank everyone involved in this 20 year search creates the apprehension of failing to acknowledge someone's help, but a list is certainly in order. So with trepidation I dare list names.

The kindness of Lois Culver from our first contact until the present has been a constant encouragement. Gary Fugate, one of the first contacts in the beginning, never failed to come through with whatever we needed and always willing to listen. And in the waning years of *Pow-Wow* (The Straight Arrow Newsletter), Jean Walton came forward to research, edit and make suggestions.

John Dunning wanted to get it right and allowed us to proof over the Straight Arrow entry in his tome, *On the Air*. Genial Ray Kemper answered so many questions and gave us a tremendous boost with his Straight Arrow memories. Dave Strivers, retired Archivist at Nabisco went the extra mile even when faced with my raised voice of occasional frustrations. Many others offered their time and talents: Barbara Watkins, Bobb Lynes & SPERDVAC (Society to Preserve and Encourage Radio Drama Variety and Comedy), Jim Scrancarelli, whose efforts led me to Fred L. Meagher's nephew which opened the way to the Meagher Special in *Alter Ego* magazine, Jerry Williams, Bruce Bingman, Ken Strobeck, Gary Egelstrom whose efforts were discovered in his papers after his death and forwarded to us by his son, Aaron Egelstrom, photographer Richard Harpster, John Morrow and Roy Thomas of *Alter Ego* magazine, Mrs. Olympia Creta, John Belfi, Bill Black, Bruce Deas, Jim Sterenko, Al Dellinges of *Near Mint* magazine, Jack French, Terry Salomonson, Jim Harmon, Leroy Brown, William Meagher, Charles (Boots) Meagher and

Robert Meagher (Fred L's brothers), Fred L. Meagher (Meagher's nephew), Ruthanne Meagher's children Rebecca and Paul Huber, and Ruthanne and Fred L. Meagher's children Don, Rick (Fred, Jr.) and Markeeta.

And many last-hour helpers; Natalie McLain, Al Hubin, John Nelson, Ted Kneebone, Stephanie Charles Eaton, Maria Hodges, Sheryn Morris, Jim Patak (Curator/ATOS Archives-Library), Santa Barbara Public Library reference desk, Jimmie Hicks, Frank Delano, Bonnie Mulcahy, Linnea Andersson-Wintle, Raylene Deck, Dr. Richard Stracke, who generously read the manuscript and offered grammatical advice, and all the *Pow-Wow* subscriber's support through the years of publishing.

And to those who contributed before passing from this life. Frank Bingman, who introduced himself one Saturday morning over the telephone by reciting in his rich voice the Straight Arrow opening. Frank continued to help with encouragement and remembrances during the early days of the *Pow-Wow* newsletter. I am sorry we did not know the questions to ask him. And there was Vin Sullivan, another one who was willing, but again we did not know what to ask. And the same with Parley Baer, John Walworth, Gardner Fox and Sheldon Stark.

Books:
*Radio and Television Sound Effects* by Robert Turnbull (Rinehart & Company 1951)
*On the Air* by John Dunning (Oxford University Press 1998)

Howard Culver carrying Lois Culver.

# Foreword

"Kah-nee-wah!!!" was the Indian war cry that drew youngsters all over America to their radios in the 1950's. One of those who listened faithfully was young Bill Harper. Bill and his family have since spent literally thousands of hours collecting Straight Arrow history, stories, and memorabilia. He is, perhaps, the foremost authority on the popular program and all those who made the program possible. He has interviewed actors, sound men, and others to obtain the many facts which are included in this book. What follows on these pages is undoubtedly the most thorough and complete picture of the Straight Arrow Radio adventures written to date.

– Lois Culver
Mrs. Howard Culver

# Introduction

Faced with the task of preparing a manuscript containing all the Straight Arrow material researched now at my fingertips, I am amazed at the odd assortment of information collected over a 20-year period. A quote from Stanislav Andreski's book *Social Sciences As Sorcery* (St. Martin Press, New York, 1972 p. 11) comes to mind "…at least 95% of research is indeed re-search for things that have been found long ago and many times since." While Andreski's remark may ring true I still feel I have the dubious honor and perhaps even the duty of gathering our Straight Arrow information together into book form for BearManor to publish making it available for you. It is an attempt at the definitive study of the Straight Arrow promotion. At the time when it aired on radio, all one had to do was wait for the next episode, not knowing what it would be, and having no idea of all that it would become for many!

Touched off by the finding of three *Straight Arrow* comics in the mid 70's, our research did not begin in earnest until 1986 with what seemed to be a very easy quest at the time, locating the Straight Arrow illustrator, Fred. L. Meagher, whose name appeared on the title page of the comic stories as well as on the covers. I could never at the time have imagined the challenges we would face, the people we would meet nor all the changes in our lifestyle that would take place. Before preparing this manuscript I reread all the copies of *Pow-Wow*, the Straight Arrow newsletter we published from Fall of 1986 until November 2001, ending with the Fred L. Meagher Special issue (partially published in *Alter Ego* #11) and the evidences of those changes were apparent. Two children would be added to our family, which already included two children, and the deaths of many involved with Straight Arrow or of their loved ones would occur, including my beloved wife Teresa in 1997. Through it all, there emerged as evident in the pages of *Pow-Wow*, a growing love for Jesus and the Church and the great realization that Jesus is all that is needed. I encourage Straight Arrow fans, as my wife and I did for years, that if you have not made an encounter with Jesus Christ, now is the hour—now is the time!

## OVERVIEW

The Straight Arrow promotion is like a jigsaw puzzle. It is hard to see the full view by looking at its various components. Often in conversation with Frank Bingman, announcer and narrator for the radio Straight Arrow, would remarked that we knew more about Straight Arrow than anybody immediately involved with the promotion at the time it actually took place. History and hindsight tend to have that advantage. However, research on a many-faceted project has the drawback that often one does one not know exactly where to look or what to ask. Often conflicting information is garnered from what historians like to refer to as "primary sources." The story of Straight Arrow has been one of sudden surprises and unexpected twists, one after another. As I write these words, I know that even though the story has been told often, there is more to be learned. During the 40s and 50s notes were not taken and records were not kept. Even later when those involved were reflecting on their history, seldom was there a stenographer present, or memories simply failed. Once this definitive source of Straight Arrow information has been published, someone, making a beginning searching for Straight Arrow will no doubt by chance rediscover, piece by piece, what took us 20 years. Hopefully they will find this book first instead.

Straight Arrow first aired nationally to millions over the Mutual Broadcasting System—some 409 stations strong—on February 7, 1949, three times weekly, Mondays 8-8:30 p.m., Tuesdays and Thursdays 5-5:30 p.m. This well orchestrated and finely tuned production had been in preparation for over a year. In late 1947 or early 1948, Sheldon Stark was engaged to script a radio show audition for McCann-Erickson Advertising Agency of New York, agent for National Biscuit Company (Nabisco), portraying an Indian as the hero. A story board was given to Stark to develop an action-packed thirty minute Western. Stark, a native New Yorker who had previously scripted The Lone Ranger, Green Hornet, Challenge of the Yukon and others for WXYZ in Detroit from 1932-1942 submitted the completed script January 5, 1948. Stark went on to write every radio episode of Straight Arrow.

Stark's script was produced in New York and presented to McCann-Erickson's client National Biscuit Company (Nabisco) for approval. Nabisco was looking for a vehicle to sell its Shredded Wheat to a younger market. The Straight Arrow concept was accepted by Nabisco, which subsequently became both sponsor and owner of the Straight Arrow property. McCann-Erickson's Hollywood office was given the responsibility of auditioning players to fill the various roles. Howard Culver, a familiar West Coast voice, was selected for the dual role of Straight Arrow/Steve Adams. Veteran actor Fred Howard (Wright) was chosen to be Packy McCloud, hired hand at Adam's Broken Bow Ranch, sidekick to both Steve Adams and Straight Arrow and the only person aware that Steve Adams was born a Comanche Indian and the legendary Straight Arrow. Gwen Delano, another seasoned player, won the role of Mesquite Molly, housekeeper of the Broken Bow. Frank Bingman rounded out the sustaining cast as narrator and announcer, while Milton Charles as organist was responsible for the music. McCann-Erickson and Nabisco gave the show a trial run on radio station KHJ of the Don Lee Network, a Mutual affiliate on the West Coast. The first show aired on May 6, 1948, and continued weekly, Tuesday evenings 8-8:30 p.m. until January 27, 1949.

The Straight Arrow show was produced in the studios of KHJ in Hollywood under the supervision of McCann-Erickson's Hollywood branch manager, J. Neil Reagan (President Ronald Reagan's older brother). The first show featured a spectacular "premium" offer—"the son of the mighty horse ridden by Straight Arrow." The horse plus tack or $1,000 would go the person submitting, with a Nabisco Shredded Wheat box-top, the name selected for Straight Arrow's golden palomino. In the meantime Straight Arrow rode from the secret cave for three months on a horse without a name! From 50,000 names, "Fury" was selected. All contestants received a Straight Arrow headband with two-red feathers for their efforts.

From Sheldon Stark's fertile imagination came the story of Steve Adams, rancher, born a Comanche Indian, orphaned and reared on the Broken Bow ranch. Later, while rescuing Packy, whom Steve did not know at the time, they were lured into the "secret cave" in Sundown Valley by a golden palomino. Steve Adams' identity as Straight Arrow, "the legendary figure spoken of around the council fires of the Comanche," was revealed. However, this idealistic story of the origin of Straight Arrow, developed over a period of time, was never aired in its entirety. When the radio show premiered the character of Straight Arrow was "full-blown." In the first episode the dual role of Steve Adams/Straight Arrow was established and, much to Steve's chagrin, alluded to by Packy even before the first trip to Sundown Valley was aired. Stark would later prepare the story of Straight Arrow's origin that was edited and printed on the inside back cover of the Injun-Uity Manual premium offered in 1951 (both versions were in the *Pow-Wow* newsletter—the condensed version reprinted in Vol. 1 No. 3, 1987, and the complete version printed for the first time in Vol. 5 No. 20, 1991).

During the 39 performances of the show on the West Coast, Nabisco in New York was preparing a premium promotion and forming a bureau called "Straight Arrow Enterprises" to license rights for various Straight Arrow merchandise items. Perhaps the most successful, popular and far-reaching promotional item was the Injun-Uity cards, three cards included free in each box of Nabisco Shredded Wheat, separating the biscuits. These cards were guides to outdoor Indian crafts and lore. The first set of 36 cards was introduced in 1949, with illustrations and information credited to Fred L. Meagher, "Indian illustrator and authority." There were three more "books" of 36 cards: Book 2 issued in 1950, Book 3 in 1951 and Book 4 in1952. Also Nabisco would offer ten Straight Arrow premium items including the headband with two-red feathers (already mentioned), an Indian war drum, golden tie clip, bandanna and slide, face ring, wrist kit, patch, nugget cave ring, Rite-A-Lite arrowhead, and Injun-Uity Manual.

Advertisers' Service Division, Inc., secured the rights to produce Straight Arrow merchandise items. John Walworth, who would eventually design many of the Straight Arrow premiums, was responsible for the creation of a full catalogue of Straight Arrow items. Listed were ten pieces; Comanche chief war drum, bandanna and slide, lollipop headband, boxed assortment of jigsaw puzzles, lollipop signal drum, framed pictures, latex mask, buffalo horn, single packages of jigsaw puzzles and coloring books. Selchow and Righter offered a board game in 1950 which was listed in its catalogue until 1956. Novel Novelties, Inc., offered two target games in 1950. A reversible Straight Arrow Indian and cowboy outfit was offered by Collegeville Flag & Mfg. Co. in 1951. Other items were listed in the Bell Syndicate's promotional flyer for the Straight Arrow strip, but many cannot be sustained by hard data, and may never have been produced.

In early 1950, Magazine Enterprises (ME) began publishing *Straight Arrow* comics in a four-color format. "See your favorite radio character!!!" was printed across the top of the first issue dated February/March 1950. The comic moved from bi-monthly status to monthly with *Straight*

*Arrow* #3. Vincent Sullivan, a former editor of National Periodical publishers of *Action Comics*, which heralded in the modern age of comics with Superman's debut in 1938, was ME's publisher. Editor for the *Straight Arrow* magazine was Raymond C. Krank. Fred L. Meagher, illustrator for many of the Straight Arrow promotional items, was the artist credited with every Straight Arrow appearance published by ME, except for two covers (issues 3 and 22) of *Straight Arrow* comics. Rounding out the Straight Arrow team at ME was Gardner F. Fox, who wrote most if not all of the Straight Arrow stories. The comic book survived the radio show by five years, ending with issue 55 dated March 1956.

In ME's *Straight Arrow* #3 was a coupon soliciting readers to respond if they wanted Straight Arrow comic strips to appear in their local newspaper. Through the efforts of Magazine Enterprises, Bell Syndicate began distributing a Straight Arrow strip, drawn by Joe Certa and John Belfi and written by Gardner Fox under the aliases of Russ Gardner and Ray Gardner. The strip lasted from July 1950 until August 4, 1951.

Before Straight Arrow went nationwide, J. Neil Reagan was replaced as executive producer by Ted Robertson, who went on to direct the remaining shows as producer and director. Ray Kemper, who worked sound at KHJ, joined McCann-Erickson, and became the assistant producer/director from late 1949 until mid 1950. The soundmen associated with the show - Tom Hanley, Dick Mobol and Bill James with Dick Burton at the sound board controls - were all on staff at KHJ.

The thrice-weekly shows ended February 2, 1950, with a Tuesday-Thursday 5 – 5:30 p.m. schedule beginning February 7, 1950, until cancellation June 21, 1951.

The Straight Arrow story, while the exact dates and the circumstances of its creation are shrouded in history, continues to draw people into nostalgic remembrances of a different time when radio was king! Families would gather around the radio to enjoy a variety of programming. Straight Arrow with its rhythmic opening and anticipation of Steve Adams' ride to Sundown Valley and the secret cave can today open a floodgate of memories of a special time and place.

It is our hope that this book will not only satisfy those who rode with their hero but might encourage others to locate copies of the show and bring Straight Arrow into the present and on into the future.

# Straight Arrow Radio

The keystone of the Nabisco Straight Arrow promotion, beginning in 1948, was of course the Straight Arrow radio show. The creative idea and premise that spawned the show continues to elude research and may be lost to posterity.

Ted Robertson, director and producer of the Straight Arrow show, was quoted in an article published in *Radio and Television Life* (1949), "The main idea we want to achieve is to help people get the correct perspective on Indian history, and in our stories we emphasize the Indian as a constructive force in our country." Robertson went on to say that the idea for a show with an Indian as the hero had originated several years prior, but for reasons unknown, was never developed. The Straight Arrow concept was not new to Robertson as he had worked on The Lone Ranger show in Detroit. Both Tonto, The Lone Ranger's Indian partner, as a hero and major character and the alter ego concept of the Lone Ranger would become influences on the development of the Straight Arrow/Steve Adams character. In the Hitching Post show (more about this later), Iron Eye Cody said, "This is the first show that has put the Indian in the correct light." In a continuing effort to support the American Indian a portion of Nabisco's commercial for May 25, 1950 Straight Arrow radio show reads; "You Straight Arrow fans can help the American Indians through the American Indian Fund. Your contributions to the Fund provide for needy Indians the country over." Followed by a New York City address. On the radio show for Thanksgiving Day, November 25, 1950 Stark tells the story of a father who hates Indians and disowns his son for befriending and Indian. The show ends on a positive note as Straight Arrow brings reconciliation between father and son and the Comanche Indians prove their worth by helping the white settlers.

What is known for sure about the inception of Straight Arrow is that

Sheldon Stark was contacted, sometime in 1947, by McCann-Erickson, Inc., ad agency for National Biscuit Company (Nabisco), to script an audition for a radio show establishing an American Indian as the main character and hero. McCann-Erickson provided what Stark called a "spring board"; however, Stark said that the character of Straight Arrow was "full blown" and an "origin" story was never scripted. The secret cave of gold and the various nuances associated with Straight Arrow were from Stark's fertile imagination. Stark submitted the finished script on January 5, 1948. A radio presentation directed by Carlos De Angelo was produced in New York for McCann-Erickson and played for Nabisco.

Nabisco approved the production and Stark finished the script for the first show, "Stage From Calvaydos," on April 5, 1948. Stark went on to complete six scripts before the show reached the air waves on May 6, 1948. According to *Sponsor* magazine (December 19, 1949), Straight Arrow's thrice-weekly showing on the Mutual Broadcasting System (MBS) represented a $1,200,000 gross annual billing. In 1948, according to data in *The 1949 Radio Annual*, Nabisco had not spent a sizable amount of advertising money with Mutual, and McCann-Erickson was not represented in Mutual's billings. Thus, the stalwart Indian, Straight Arrow, was not only on the trail of justice but he represented millions of dollars for Mutual.

This radio show that would eventually generate millions of dollars was given an 18 week trial run on Mutual's West Coast affiliate, the Don Lee Network, and was produced at station KHJ in Hollywood. McCann-Erickson turned the production over to its Hollywood office, under the management of J. Neil Reagan (President Ronald Reagan's older brother), a Senior Producer in McCann-Erickson's Radio-TV Division. Reagan himself was the Straight Arrow radio show's producer and director. Auditions for the show found Howard Culver cast in the main role of Straight Arrow/Steve Adam, Fred Howard (Wright) as Packy McCloud, friend to both Straight Arrow and Steve Adams and the only person that knew their dual identity, Gwen Delano as Mesquite Molly, housekeeper of the Broken Bow Ranch and Frank Bingman, announcer and narrator, who played a pivotal role in developing the legend of Straight Arrow. The overwhelming success of the Tuesday evening 8-8:30 p.m. show, accounting for a 10% increase in sales of Nabisco Shredded Wheat on the West Coast and receipt of 50,000 box tops and names for Straight Arrow's golden palomino, extended the show for an additional 21 episodes for a total of 39 shows over the Don Lee Network and a berth in Mutual's nationwide network.

By February 7, 1949, when Straight Arrow reached millions of listeners over the Mutual Broadcasting System nationwide, the program was well-honed. The variances of the opening and the cave sequence had been ironed out and all the actors were comfortable in their respective roles. The massive promotional efforts of Nabisco's 28 district sales offices in key cities and 241 branches, as well as the 409 Mutual stations, were set into motion. According to *Sponsor* magazine, the show quickly became the "top-rated kid show, with a spectacular Nielsen rating of 7.5 as well as moving into the 8th slot in Nielsen's Top Ten national listings, marking the first time a children's show had cracked that select bracket."

Sometime before the Straight Arrow radio show reached nationwide attention, Reagan became the show's executive producer and Ted Robertson was hired as director/producer. Ray Kemper, soundman for KHJ, joined McCann-Erickson as the assistant director/producer (the two titles being used interchangeable) for Straight Arrow.

As a part of all the promotional hailing Straight Arrow move to Mutual's nationwide hook-up, Mutual presented a "Straight Arrow Pow-Wow" radio program originating from the Hitching Rail theater in Hollywood, California, on Hollywood Boulevard. According to bibliographer Donald Morgan, you could view three old Westerns each show time at the Hitching Rail, but what he remembered most was "…pegs on the wall; you used to have to hang up your cap gun before you went in!" The program, hosted by Ben Alexander, featured western stars Johnny Mack Brown, Jim Wakely, Iron Eye Cody and Whip Wilson. The show concluded with the crowning of Little Chief Straight Arrow (Ralph Hoppe) and his Princess Straight Arrow (Honey Hollingsworth). However, in all the hurrah there was no Straight Arrow or any of the cast members. Interestingly the promotional ad mentioned Straight Arrow on-the-air Mondays, with no mention of the three-day-a-week schedule that prevailed.

Submitting a Nabisco Shredded Wheat boxtop and a name for Straight Arrow's horse initiated the first give-away offer. Of the 50,000 names sent the name "Fury" was selected and Straight Arrow rode out of the secret cave using Fury's name for the first time in radio show, "The Iron Horse," (#12) July 22, 1948. The person submitting the winning name had the choice of a golden palomino pony with tack or $1,000. Howard Culver's widow, Lois Culver, wrote on March 1, 1986 that "when Howard's daughter Pam was a teenager she mentioned to us casually that in the early days of Straight Arrow, when they were looking for a name for Fury and held a contest (the prize being a palomino), Pam's good friend won the prize for the name (because she thought he ran like fury)."

According to *Sponsor* magazine, the winner took the money. For every name submitted, the sender received a Straight Arrow two red feather head band. The head band (slightly modified) was again offered when the show went nationwide, February 7, 1949, and this time 500,000 boxtops and requests were received. In an article in *Life* magazine (March 14, 1949) it was reported: "Premium merchandising is at an all-time high, last year (1948) 8,000 firms distributed one billion dollars worth of premiums to help sell an estimated $5 billion worth of products." The article reported "a return of half a million orders isn't even colossal." The head band was followed by the first self-liquidating premium, the Indian war drum. It pulled well, but not up to the head band. This was followed with the Straight Arrow gold tie clip. According to R. Steward Boyd, advertising manager for Nabisco's cereal division, in *Sponsor* magazine, "this lure was 'terrible'" and was "one of the factors that prompted Nabisco's decision to interrupt its sponsorship." Straight Arrow remained on Mutual as a sustainer for 13 weeks before Nabisco resumed in September 1949. For a show to remain on radio without sponsorship was not unusual, especially if it was popular. The plan would be for another advertiser to pick up the tab, but with Straight Arrow, it would have had to be worked out with Nabisco as Nabisco owned exclusive rights to the show.

It was also noted in *Sponsor* magazine that the Monday 8-8:30 p.m. show, according to Nabisco, "…attracted many adult listeners…" Interestingly the shows heard during the 13 weeks mentioned above were in the late Monday time slot. Straight Arrow returned to the three-day-per-week schedule following a special Sunday broadcast on September 18, 1949, "Buffalo Hunt" (not numbered in the radio log). A show with the same title and characters had been aired on February 10, 1949 (show #42), however with a different cast. On February 7, 1950 (show #170), the show went to a twice weekly format, Tuesdays and Thursdays 5-5:30 p.m., until going off the air June 21, 1951 (show #292). During the summer break, September 12 (show #211) to September 21 (show #214), 1950, there were two weeks of repeat shows. In Stark's ledger, which he used as a means to keep up with the submittal dates of finished work, there is a notation at that time of an interest at Decca Records in issuing a recording of Straight Arrow. To date research has not located such a recording.

The opening signature and the cave sequence changed very little over the duration of the radio show. Steve Adams' voice deepened slightly into Straight Arrow's voice. Once on the trail of justice the stories raced pell-mell to a spellbinding conclusion.

Nabisco and/or McCann Erickson created Nabisco Shredded Wheat commercials so as not to interfere with the action. The lead commercial was worked into the opening signature with Milton Charles' organ created the pulsating sounds of Indian drums while Frank Bingman rhythmically spelled N A B I S C O and declaimed the jingle;

> "Nabisco is the name to know
> For a breakfast you can't beat
> Eat Nabisco Shredded Wheat."

Excellent acting, strong scripts and superb sound effects were some of the obvious elements insuring the success of the Straight Arrow radio show. But underlying these traits were subtleties—good direction, imaginative and effective promotional schemes and a genuine interest in making Straight Arrow more than a variation on Western themes with an Indian as the main character—that furthered enhanced the show. Ted Robertson and Ray Kemper spent time studying the folkways of Western Indians, and for his scripting Sheldon Stark was awarded honorary membership in the Iroquois Confederation. Senator Dennis Chavez of New Mexico read an appreciation and tribute of the show into the Congressional Record on Indian Day, September 23, 1949.

## SHELDON STARK

The person most responsible for the spirit of radio's Straight Arrow was writer extraordinary, Sheldon Stark. He wrote every Straight Arrow radio script as well as the "origin story," which was edited and reproduced on the inside back cover of the Injun-Uity Manual, a 1951 Nabisco premium (both versions were published in *Pow-Wow* issues 3 and 20). The cave sequence, that moment in the show that listeners eagerly anticipated, was created from Stark's imagination.

Born in Brooklyn, New York, September 7, 1909, Sheldon Stark attended Lincoln School, an experimental school of the Teachers College of Columbia College. In 1930 he graduated from Dartmouth College with a major in psychology. In 1994, Stark wrote, "I was a lead writer on the *Jack*

*'O Lantern*, Dartmouth's humor magazine. I was a writer and sure my life was gonna be a snap. Some snap. What snapped was the economy; the year I tossed my tassel and entered the wide, wide world was—you got it—1930, year one of the Great Depression. It took three years to finally sell something - a cartoon idea to a new magazine, *The New Yorker*, for which I got five dollars. Thank all the gods that be I've done better since…"

Stark found a job with a small advertising agency proofing radio scripts. He found many of the scripts poorly written and decided to try his hand at scripting, producing three or four. He adapted a Stephen Vincent Benét story for the Columbia Radio Workshop. In 1939 he joined WXYZ in Detroit as an assistant to Fran Striker writing scripts for The Lone Ranger, Green Hornet, Challenge of the Yukon and whatever else they required. In 1941, Stark returned to his hometown. In the late 40's he was approached by McCann-Erickson Advertising Agency to write an audition radio script with an American Indian as a hero. The agency gave some ideas as a "spring board." Stark finished the script and turned it over to McCann-Erickson on January 5, 1948. Years later Stark was confronted by the fact that Straight Arrow had many nuances associated with radio's Lone Ranger. Stark did not deny this; in fact, he said that McCann-Erickson/Nabisco were looking for a Lone Range type show and he "did a little swipe on The Lone Ranger." A New York studio produced the script under the guidance of veteran director Carlos De Angelo. Stark went on to write an additional 288 Straight Arrow scripts for a total of 289. He reported he never saw any of the shows produced however he did communicated with director Ted Robertson on the telephone on several occasions.

A note dated June 6, 1950, on Stark's legal ledger, which was used to keep track of monies received for writing as well as percent to his agent, mentioned a deal with issuing a Straight Arrow show on Decca Records. A notation of "N.G." appears, which could have meant "no good/go." To date there is no evidence that a Decca recording was ever produced.

On March 6, 1956, Stark received a letter from Ivan R. Wainer, attorney at law, in Beverly Hills, California asking about the availability of the Straight Arrow series for a television production. Stark responded that he was "very interested" and was turning the request over to his agent. Within a month Stark sent a letter to Farish Jenkins at McCann-Erickson, New York, explaining that he had gotten several "indefinite queries" concerning the Straight Arrow property. From the letter it is apparent that Stark had talked with Stu Boyd at Nabisco regarding the possible optioning of Straight Arrow for movies and television and was asking Jenkins "whether the position has changed." As further discussion was to be made at lunch one can only guess at what the "position" may have been.

Sheldon Stark was an engrossed and prolific writer with a career that spanned his entire adult life. He churned out more than 500 scripts for both radio and television. He wrote several novels, including *Too Many Sinners* in the Ace Double series (D-81) published by Ace Books, Inc. (New York, NY) in 1954. He produced in every medium: printed page, movies, radio, TV and stage plays. His collection in the Division of Rare Books and Special Collections at The University of Wyoming, certainly not all his works, reveals numerous accepted works as well as many uncompleted projects.

In 1933 he was cartoon editor of the first commercial comic book, *More Fun*. He wrote many well known comic strips of the 30's: *Jack Armstrong - All American Boy*, *Robin Hood* to name a couple. Twice he was involved in the creation of comic strips drawn by well known illustrators: *Inspector Wade* (1935-1947) with Lyman Anderson and *Jet Scott* (1953-1955) with Batman artist, Jerry Robinson. His radio credits include the ones named elsewhere as well as other popular productions: Grand Central Station, Amos and Andy, Superman, The Listening Post, etc.

In 1951, just before Straight Arrow went of the air, Stark had submitted an audition for Rocky King, Detective, an early production of Dumont Television. He went on to write a total of 17 episodes for this short-lived feature. He wrote for every major TV series: The Fugitive, Batman, The Waltons, Wagon Train, Rawhide, the Man from Uncle, Mission Impossible, Mod Squad, Hawaiian Eye, Quincy, etc. Stark's scripting efforts on Straight Arrow garnered a membership in the Iroquois Confederation and a mention of the show in the Congressional Records (Vol. 95, No. 177 page 13447) on American Indian Day, September 23, 1949.

Stark moved from New York to Pacific Palisades, where he was co-founder of Theatre Palisades and taught screenwriting at UCLA and Santa Monica College. He died February 6, 1997.

## HOWARD CULVER

Howard Brasfield Culver, Jr., who rode the radio air waves as the great Comanche War Chief Straight Arrow, was far afield of his original plans to become a physician. Born June 2, 1919, in a rural area near Fort Collins, Colorado, to Howard Culver, Sr. and Mabel Ogden, Culver's publicity acknowledge him

as a knowledgeable rider, learning his skills on the family's ranch. Actually the Culver family moved to Pasadena, California when he was a "tiny tot." At school Culver and his sister, Cora Jane, joined a dance group which did exhibition ballroom and adagio dancing. "This may have given him the 'performing bug,'" Lois Culver, widow to Howard Culver, recalled. From Pasadena the Culver family moved to Los Angeles. In high school Culver was active in the school theater group, not only acting, but assisting in building sets and doing the many other activities involved in staging a play. It was during his senior year that Culver would have an opportunity on Los Angeles' Boys' Day to "work" professionally in an area of his interest. Culver, chosen to represent the theater department, was invited to have a speaking part on a real radio show on CBS in Hollywood. His deep, mature voice and professional mannerism in this small part caused the producer to offer him additional shows. For six weeks, or thereabout, Culver was called once a week for small parts on CBS radio. He earned his first pay check quite unexpectedly as he did not know he was to be paid for "having fun." When he graduated in 1936, college seemed a long way off as it was necessary for him to help contribute to his sister's college tuition as their father was not physically well. Culver worked various jobs and in the summer of 1939, while working in the laundry at Yosemite National Park, he met a young lady, Maxine (Miki) Born from nearby Merced. They were married in March, 1939, and divorced in 1949 after being separated for several years. Culver and Maxine had a daughter, Pamela. During this time Culver had begun a career in radio working various assignments. He broadcast many shows at KFI– NBC in Los Angeles including a nightly program where he read poetry with organ background. He had originated the ideas while in San Francisco and was asked to reprise it at KFI. At first called Stairway to the Stars, it was later changed to A Joy Forever. At KFI he met national Traffic Manager Lois Hayes, and they were married in 1950 and in 1953 had twin daughters, Patti (Patricia) and Kathi (Katherine). Shortly before the marriage Culver, who had appeared as radio's last Ellery Queen (The Adventures of Ellery Queen , 1947-48), was chosen to play the dual role of Straight Arrow and Steve Adam on the Mutual Broadcasting System from KHJ in Hollywood. While in the lead role of Straight Arrow, Culver still found time to take roles in other productions. He was the announcer/narrator for Chandu, The Magician (1948-1950), which has been remembered through the years for the White King Soap commercials. He was asked to cut a demonstration disk for a new western lead, Mark (later Matt) Dillon, in a show called Gunsmoke. Culver's voice was chosen, but his contract with the Straight Arrow production would not allow him playing another lead. Thus it was given to William Conrad, who had also auditioned. When Straight Arrow ended June 21, 1951, Culver continued in radio co-starring with Mercedes McCambridge in Defense Attorney (1951-1952) as well as others. In a letter dated July 25, 1951, Culver was asked if he was willing to continue his role of Straight Arrow in a new production. The writer was a Wilbur Stark of New York City. The letter outlined a pay scale and a line that indicated a contract would be forthcoming the "first week of September." Culver responded in August 1951 that he was excited about the possibilities and that he agreed with the pay scale, but mentioned he needed approval by the American Federation of Radio Artists (AFRA). In this same letter Culver would make a passionate appeal to have Ted Robertson continue as producer/director.

With the tremendous growth in television production and sales of television sets Culver made his TV debut in 1949 on KHJ-TV in a local drama series. Later he appeared in the premiere of Gunsmoke (September 10, 1955), as Howie, the desk clerk at the Dodge House. In 1972 an article on Gunsmoke in *TV Guide* (Vol.20, No 12) listed him as a member of "Gunsmoke's stock company." Culver worked many other TV shows such as Dragnet, Perry Mason, Marcus Welby, M.D., to name a few. He worked both as actor and voice over.

Culver took a hiatus from radio due to the loss of hearing in one ear. He bought one of Frank Bingman's hobby shops. But he returned to the air after successful surgery gave back his hearing. He joined the news staff at KLAC–Los Angles. Culver performed in several movies with his most prominent role in Jack Webb's - *30* - (1959), a movie depicting a day in the newsroom of a newspaper.

In 1980 Culver retired, appearing in local stage productions or acting in roles he found interesting.

On the way home from a three-week tour of China, Culver contracted a respiratory illness and died August 5, 1985. He was buried at sea off Point Fermin (out of San Pedro, California).

## FRED HOWARD (WRIGHT)

Fred Howard (Wright) appeared in every episode of the Straight Arrow radio show as Packy McCloud, side-kick to Steve Adams/Straight Arrow and the only person knowing the dual identity of Straight Arrow and Steve Adams. Why Fred Howard dropped his last name "Wright" in favor of Howard has been speculated on by several radio personalities and the most plausible explanation being that there was already someone in the entertainment industry with the same name. Howard was born September 30, 1896, in San Diego, California to former Nebraskan. As a youngster he wrote verse and was a natural mimic. He had a tenor voice and was attracted by the musical stage. In San Francisco during the early 1930s he teamed with eastern Nat Vincent forming a song writing team that would find moderate success, especially on the west coast. Vincent was a child musical prodigy from New York City via Virginia/Kentucky. In New York Vincent collaborated with two others to write "I'm Forever Blowing Bubbles." Howard and Vincent entered radio as a harmony team on station KFRC's production, Blue Monday Jamboree. During their time slot they introduced comic routines and sang. Later at KFI in Los Angeles they developed and wrote songs for the well known West Coast group the Beverly Hill Billies. During this period they recorded songs as The Happy Chappies on Columbia Records. M. M. Cole Publishing Co published *Greatest Collection of Outdoor Songs* of the Happy Chappies in 1935. The song "When the Bloom Is On The Sage (Round Up time

In Texas)" was covered by many groups and singers, including such a notable as Bing Crosby. The music for "When The Bloom Is On The Sage," credited to Fred Howard, was used for the theme song of the Tom Mix radio show. The Happy Chappies became "Pacific Coast Radio Favorites" appearing on KMPC in Beverly Hills and KNX, Hollywood. The above mention song and "I'd Like To Be In Texas For The Round Up In The Spring" continue to entertain fans of cowboy songs. Fred Howard began appearing in radio programs in the early 1940s and in 1948 landed the costarring role in Straight Arrow. Later he would appear on The Saint as well as writing 18 weeks of that show. He also appeared on Wild Bill Hickok. He played Lefty on Aunt Mary, Uncle Avery on Gasoline Alley and eight years as D. Premberton Toohey on Ma Perkins. As a writer he did eight months of Mystery Is My Hobby and four months of Danger Dr. Danfield. Conrad Binyon, who worked with Howard, remarked, "I knew about him (Fred Howard) from having seen his picture in the Chicago section of Lew Lauria's National Radio Artists Directory." However his travel and his work at various locations has not been fully documented.

THE HAPPY CHAPPIES
Pacific Coast Radio Favorites
KMPC—Beverly Hills    KNX—Hollywood

In the early 50's Howard, using the name Howard Wright, would be credited with appearing in a string of TV productions beginning with Adventures of Wild Bill Hickock (1951), and including such as Annie Oakley, The Real McCoys, Frontier Doctor, Wagon Train, 77 Sunset Strip, Gunsmoke, Bonanza, The Wild Wild West. Howard (Wright) was credited with a list of 29 movies from *Last of the Pony Riders* (1953) to *The Legend of Frank Woods* (1977). His most notable role was in the Audie Murphy movie, *To Hell and Back* (1955), as Mr. Ben Houston. Most of the roles were small parts and most without credit.

Fred Howard Wright died in La Crescenta (Los Angeles) July 2, 1990.

## GWEN DELANO

Gwen Delano was born Gwendoline Maude Delaney on November 24, 1881 in Omaha, Nebraska. A veteran actress, she successfully auditioned the role of Mesquite Molly, a major character, and joined the cast of Straight Arrow. Mesquite Molly, billed as the housekeeper of the Broken Bow ranch on the radio program as well as in the comics and the daily newspaper strips, was involved in many of the adventures. From the information gathered it appears she never suspected Steve Adams of being Straight Arrow, despite the obvious fact that Packy was side-kick to both men and that after the mysterious disappearance of Steve, Straight Arrow would appear or vice-versa. Mesquite Molly's first appearance was in the fourth show, "The Dead Man Speaks," May 27, 1948. She appeared in only about half of the Straight Arrow radio productions.

In the *1949 Standard Radio and Television Directory* (Vol. 2) Delano was listed as having appeared on radio for 18 years in New York, Chicago and Hollywood in such notable roles as Grandmother in Junior Miss, Mesquite Molly on Straight Arrow as well as roles on Dr. Christian, Jack Benny, Phil Harris, Railroad Hour etc. Under the heading "Stage" she is credited with 40 years of acting with "20 years supporting our best stars." It was recorded in her obituary that she had worked with the Dolly Sisters and Richard Bennett, famous names associated with Vaudeville. The *New York Times* obituary for Gwen Delano noted that she helped organize the American Federation of Radio Artists (AFRA) and later become its executive secretary as well as appearing on The Lone Ranger radio show for seven years. Dick Osgood in his book *WYXIE - Wonderland* (Bowling Green University Popular Press 1981) mentioned a Gwen Delany (as Osgood wrote, Delany pronounced her last name, DeL-A-H not DeL-A-Y), an actress who got her start as a maid in WXYZ's radio production, Ann Worth Housewife. Osgood went on to write that Delany, who acted in many other shows at WXYZ, was instrumental in the formation of the Detroit chapter of AFRA and eventually elected its first Executive Secretary. According to Osgood her radio work dwindled due to her union involvement thus in 1941 she moved to California, where she continued in radio. Osgood wrote, "Gwen Delany found no great degree of happiness in California, jobs were scarce, she no longer was young; and she was not in the best of health." Some obituaries mentioned Delano's appearances on television's Dragnet and radio's The Lux Radio Theater and Jack Benny Show.

The Gwen Delano of the *New York Times* obituary parallels the Gwen Delany written of in Osgood's book *WYXIE - Wonderland* confirming that they are one and the same even though the listing for Delano in the *1949 Standard Radio and Television Directory* did not mention Detroit. It also should be noted that both Ted Robertson, director and producer of Straight Arrow, and Sheldon Stark, writer of all Straight Arrow radio shows, were both at WXYZ Detroit during the same period as Gwen Delano/Delany. Stark, on a SPERVAC Convention panel in 1989, remarked he thought his union involvement may have led to the cancellation of Straight Arrow radio.

Gwen Delano (Delany - Delaney) died November 20, 1954, four days prior to her 73rd birthday.

## FRANK BINGMAN

When Frank Bingman successfully auditioned for the announcer/narrator position of the new radio series, Straight Arrow, at KHJ in Hollywood, little did he know his working with the star of that show would develop into a life-long friendship. Bingman recalled that Howard Culver, a short, red bearded man, was sitting in a corner knitting Argyle socks when introduced. "Straight Arrow" knitting socks struck a responsive cord with Frank as he, too, was a knitter - "closet variety." Bruce Bingman, Frank Bingman's son, related that knitting was one of several inventive ways his father used to stop smoking by keeping his hands and mind occupied with something to keep his mind off of cigarettes. The two men were drawn together and soon became close friends, sharing their lives after Straight Arrow, both professionally and socially.

Frank Bingman was born on a farm between Athens and Nelsonville, Ohio, April 9, 1914. He dreamed of a future in electronics, but upon completion of high school he received a "scholarship" to the Cincinnati Drama School. At the school he designed sets and acted. The school led directly to his radio career, as the local radio station would often use students for bit parts. Once Frank performed as a coroner, saying five words and netting $5.00. "One dollar per word, that was more than I had ever made at any job," he explained.

At Drama School he met his future wife, Madelyn, who directed the entire dance department. He thought her much older than he due to her professional responsibilities. After "several weeks I found out that I was the older person." Madelyn and Frank subsequent marriage lasted over 50 years.

Bingman worked WLW and in 1935 joined WKRC, Cincinnati, where Madelyn had a two hour morning show. Frank believes she might have been the first female DJ (disc jockey).

The Bingmans moved to California in 1937. Madelyn found work immediately in the dance business. Bingman did frequent movie and radio work. By World War II Madelyn had her own dance studio and company and Bingman freelanced 21 radio shows however, he "lost [his] mind and enlisted in the military service." Frank reminisced "that in the Signal Corps, I was a so-called radar 'expert' attached to various groups for a series of island-hopping landings form New Guinea to the Philippines."

With the electronic knowledge gained in the Corps, Bingman sought employment in the electronic field upon discharge from the service. He found no work and returned to broadcasting, landing a classical DJ job.

Three years after Straight Arrow ended, Bingman left radio and opened a hobby shop, which Culver later bought, after the Bingmans had opened a second shop. The hobby shop was the outcome of another "hand and mind" project to keep from smoking. Bingman would bring his models to work, creating considerable interest, especially by Culver, who also was into model building.

However Bingman returned to radio and became a TV news director. In 1972 he "retired" from full-time broadcasting, working some weekends doing trailers for 20th Century Fox and occasional cameo appearances on various television shows. "My longest running job was not broadcasting, per se, but for 20th Century Fox. For thirteen years I did 'trailers' for every picture released through Fox. These trailers were used in theaters to announce the next week's features. These 'coming attractions' were also used on radio and television."

Bruce Bingman told Pow-Wow a humorous story of one of his father's TV appearances. "Both my dad and Howard had been called to do a Gunsmoke episode. Howard appeared in his semi-permanent role as Howie the hotel clerk and dad was cast as a cowpoke in the background. As the scene unfolded, Marshall Dillion (James Arness) rushed in pushing and shoving people and furniture, grabbed Howie (Howard Culver) by the shirt front and asked him where the bad guys had taken Miss Kitty. Now as you recall, Arness is a BIG guy and when he rushed in he flipped a table over on dad's toe, smashing it; his grab of Howard included shirt and chest hair. Howard's grimace and shout of agony as he pointed 'that-a-way' were more than acting!"

Later the Bingmans moved east to Warrenton, Virginia where Bingman became a viable part of the local theater. In 1986 Bingman was critically acclaimed for his role as Henry Drummond in the play *Inherit the Wind*.

The announcer/narrator role on Straight Arrow made Bingman an integral part of the cast. His delivery of the opening set the mood of the series. His linkage of dialogue moved the action smoothly through time and scene changes as well as the commercial breaks. Bingman elevated the pivotal point of the Straight Arrow script—the cave scenario—to a fine art. Bingman's voice brought excitement to the mystical transformation of Steve Adams to Straight Arrow in the cave of gold.

Bingman's career from 1934 through his "first retirement" found him as an actor at WLW, Cincinnati, from 1934-1937 and a staff announcer with WKRC, Cincinnati, a CBS outlet, during the same time period. After his move to California he was a staff announcer for KHJ, Hollywood, from 1937-1939 and a staff announcer for the NBC station in Hollywood from 1939 through 1941. He freelanced many shows doing various commercials, especially the "thirty second 'spot tags,' for instance when Don Wilson finished selling Jell-O on the Jack Benny Show, I would do a thirty second spot for Jell-O Pudding,—I never got name credit, but I did collect a few dollars."

After World War II, Bingman did Cavalcade of America, My Friend Irma, Joan Davis Comedy Hour and Straight Arrow to name a few.

Frank Bingman's beautiful voice was silenced August 21, 1988 in Warrenton, Virginia.

## MILTON CHARLES

Harry Bartell, who played Randy Culver in the first Straight Arrow radio show, Stage From Calvaydos, May 6, 1948 wrote in his on going old time radio essay, *Struts and Frets*, "The radio actor didn't have the luxury of long rehearsal time or unlimited takes, but he had two advantages that an actor in film couldn't duplicate: live sound and music. Sometimes they were quite limited, especially in music where the Hammond Organ constituted the orchestra. Still, musicians like Milton Charles, Ivan Ditmars, Gaylord Carter were able to bring a strong sense of dramatic color to a dead studio. The organ 'sting,' a sharp accent at a very dramatic moment became a must in action drama or soaps and it was easy for these musicians to write or even improvise background music for narration or mood scenes." Bartell's assessment of the sound and music involved in a production certainly describes the vitality organist Milton Charles brought to the Straight Arrow show right from the opening "sting" indicating an arrow in flight and then the thud of the arrow into wood while Frank Bingman drew out and accenting the words "Straight Arrow!"

Milton Charles was born at San José, California, May 8, 1897, into a musical family. He was playing the piano at the age of 7 and was a church organist at 13. In 1912, at 15, he playing at the Jewel Theater in San Francisco and later he was an assistant at the Million Dollar Theatre, an opulent theater on Broadway in Los Angeles. He then followed organist Jesse Crawford at the Miller's California Theatre in Los Angeles.

Moving to Chicago, Charles made several recordings, one at the Gunn School. In 1924 he recorded live at the Tivoli Theatre in Chicago, Illinois. This two-sided recording for Columbia Records is considered by some to be the first ever recordings of a theatre organ. Charles is credited with Wayne King and

Jack Yellen on writing the popular song, "Hula Lo." Charles once remarked to King, who played saxophone in the Tivoli orchestra, that he was going to write a song based on King's warm-up phrase of about three notes. When Yellen, who owned a music publishing house, approached Charles to write a tune Charles used the three notes and with Yellen lyrics, "Hula Lo" was created. Charles had King cut into the deal for a third of the royalties. During the same time period Charles and Sam Stept wrote the music to "Back Home in Illinois" with words by Coleman Goestz.

In 1929, when the Metropolitan Threatre in Los Angels reopened as the Paramount Theater, Charles was offered the position of chief organist.

Returning to the east Charles, performed at the Mastbaum Theatre in Philadelphia from 1930-1934.

In 1936 Charles returned to Chicago, where he shifted from theater work to radio work as a staff member of WBBM - CBS. He returned to California after the outbreak of World War II, where he continued with CBS at Columbia Square, Hollywood, over KNX. Here he developed a mid-afternoon show, Moments of Mid-Afternoon Music, and a night production, Prelude to Midnight, where frequently he sang to his own accompaniment.

Charles performed on a variety of radio shows, including Tapestries Of Life 1940-1945; Dr. Christian (10 years - 1940s - 1950s where J. Neil Reagan was director); Jeff Regan, Investigator 1948; Rocky Jordan. 1949; Straight Arrow 1948-1951; The Roy Rogers Show 1951-1952; Yours Truly, Johnny Dollar 1953.

It is known that Charles did recordings for RCA, Columbia, Brunswick, and Autograph. He played the organ on Guy Lombardo's recording of "High Upon a Hilltop" in 1929.

Billed as "Milton Charles, the singing organist," Charles was musically involved with a Vitaphone (early talkies films 1925-1935) production titled "Spooney Melodies" (Cryin' for the Carolines).

The American Theatre Organ Society (ATOS) acknowledged Milton Charles, in 1978, for his contribution to enhancing the public interest in the theatre organ by selecting him Organist of the Year as well as election into ATOS's Hall of Fame.

Milton Charles died in Corona, California, November 1, 1991.

## TED ROBERTSON

When the Straight Arrow radio show premiered May 6, 1948, the director was J. Neil Reagan, the office manager of McCann-Erickson Agency's Hollywood office. Reagan, faced with Agency activity, sought a replacement for himself. He interviewed many prospects and finally settled on Ted Robertson, of whom Ray Kemper remarked, "Neil…was never disappointed in that choice."

John Edward (Ted) Robertson was born in Michigan September 26, 1912. Ray Kemper raised doubt about Robertson's birth year as 1912. Kemper recalled that he once asked Robertson his age and was told by Robertson that he was nine years older than Kemper, who was born in 1923, making the birth year 1914. Dick Osgood, *WYXIE Wonderland (an unauthorized 50 year diary of WXYZ Detroit)* 1981, reminisces that Robertson worked a summer company touring at night throughout Michigan and in the afternoons worked with James Jewell. Jewell later went to work with WXYZ, and Robertson, who returned to Detroit at the tour's end and found himself with nothing to do, contacted Jewell who offered him a job in sound effects without pay. A year later, Robertson, who was living with his uncle and aunt literally ran out of money for fare to the studio. Jewell offered him a paying job and Robertson joined the staff, acting the role of Tadpole Teddy on Kiddie Karnival and as announcer on Ann Worth, Housewife. In sound effects, Osgood credited Robertson with assisting in the development of the "bee" sound for the Green Hornet show and with Fred Flowerday inventing the sound for Jack Benny's Maxwell automobile, which eventually was replaced by the talented voice of Mel Blanc. Osgood attributes Robertson's leaving WXYZ and Detroit over an incident with Brace Beemer. At the time the future Lone Ranger, Beemer, was in management and a narrator on The Lone Ranger radio show. Robertson, now an assistant dramatic director was involved with directing The Lone Ranger rehearsals. Beemer often arrived late much to Robertson's chagrin and on several occasions they had harsh words. Osgood went on to state that Robertson threatened to fire Beemer from the show. There were similar incidents and in 1939 it was Robertson who was fired. He and several staff members (Gwen Delany [Delano] was one) were involved in the formation of a branch of the American Federation of Radio Artists (AFRA). The union was not popular with management. Robertson went to Chicago and joined the staff of CBS, where he is credited with bringing Mike Wallace to the attention of the network. During the war years 1941-1945 Robertson directed American Women (drama) and Service To The Front (produced in behalf of U.S. Army). Osgood related that Robertson joined Compton Advertising, Inc. (agents for Proctor and Gamble in the late 1940s) and became vice president and west coast manager for radio and TV programming. The reliability of Osgood's reflections on Robertson's life after leaving Detroit comes into question here. Robertson did join Compton, but it was apparently after the Straight Arrow show; however, Osgood may have been correct and Robertson rejoined Compton after Straight Arrow. Also it should be noted that Osgood places Robertson death day as being July 14, 1975 at the age of 55, the date does not agree with the Robertson's obituary.

The exact date for Robertson's involvement with Straight Arrow radio is not available, but certainly it was soon after the show started over the Don Lee Network. By February 7, 1949, when the show aired nationwide over the Mutual Broadcasting System Robertson was the director and producer working under Reagan, who continued as the executive director. Ray Kemper, who was a member of the sound crew at KHJ, joined McCann-Erickson Agency as writer/director and was assigned as assistant director (assistant producer) of Straight Arrow. During the Straight Arrow tenure Robertson demonstrated a keen interest in the American Indians, and in August 1949 he and Kemper traveled to the Inter-Tribal Indian Ceremonial in Gallup, New Mexico. Here Robertson and Kemper recorded interviews, dance music and the rich variety of sounds of this annual event. Kemper took photographs. Their hope to use the sounds on Straight Arrow was never realized, but a two part series, Straight Arrow's Brother, appeared in *Radio & Television Life* magazine (October 23 and 30, 1949) written by Robertson with photographs by Kemper as well as a radio production, Song Of The Tom-Tom. This broadcast was a documentary offer on September 23, 1949, American Indian Day, starring Burl Ives, Kay Starr, Roy Rogers, Dale Evans, Chief Thundercloud, The Riders of the Purple Sage and Honorable Judge H. B. Johnson, a full-blooded Indian and Jurist of the Oklahoma Supreme Court, as well as both Ted Robertson and Ray

Kemper. It was this Mutual Broadcasting production that led Senator Dennis Chavez, United State Senator from New Mexico to speak about Straight Arrow from the floor of the Senate and thus his remarks were recorded in the Congressional Records (Vol. 95, No. 177 p. 13477) on the very day the show aired.

Robertson joined McCann-Erickson Agency after Straight Arrow went off the air June 21, 1951, which is the main point of the Straight Arrow radio show "spoof." The "spoof" which makes fun of "those bales of hay" (Nabisco shredded wheat biscuits) is thought to be, by some, a response to the "sudden" cancellation of Straight Arrow show. With McCann-Erickson, Robertson was director for the Dr. Christian (1952) radio show. Ray Kemper wrote of seeing Robertson occasionally, the last time in the 1970s, and learned that Robertson and his wife, June, an artist, had moved to Santa Barbara, California, where he was semi-retired. Kemper went on to say, "Ted Robertson was an important part of my career in my earlier years in radio. He was warm, friendly and completely unselfish." This admiration for Robertson was mirrored by Howard Culver in response to an enquiry by a Wilbur Stark of New York City to Culver's availability to continue acting the dual role of Straight Arrow. In Culver's reply he referred to Robertson and wrote, "…you know that he [Robertson] fell in love with the show and Indians in general from almost the first day he was on it." Howard continued, "…I'm sure that with Robertson directing all concerned—cast, music, sound, everyone—will feel much easier in production and more confident of doing a good job. It's just that Robertson has that certain extra something that makes for good commercial radio production."

After leaving McCann-Erickson Robertson joined Compton Advertising, Inc., where he remained until his death on April 5, 1975.

## RAY KEMPER

Cordial Ray Kemper was born Raymond Clinton Kemper, December 23, 1923, in Lankershim, California, in what is now known as North Hollywood. He attended area schools and in the midst of the world of movies he quickly developed a determined interest to become an actor. It was natural for an aspiring young novice to be open to all and any form of acting. Radio personalities were listed as actors and actresses, so to be near the world of acting Kemper, upon graduation from high school in January 1942, found a job as a page with radio station KHJ. A few weeks into the job he auditioned and got a night shift announcer position while continuing screen testing for movie roles. Kemper's draft status, "1A," caused concern with producers and indeed a year later he was drafted into the Army, spending three years "with a few million other guys." Returning in 1946, Kemper found his slot at KHJ had been filled. The station was obligated to rehire him at his old position; however, Kemper opted not to demand his old job. KHJ offered him work in sound effects, about which he knew little, but they offered to train him. In 1947 he wrote 12 to 13 scripts under the name N. Clint Reynolds for the series The Count of Monte Cristo. Later Kemper would develop ideas and write scripts for Gunsmoke and Have Gun Will Travel, to name a few.

In 1948 KHJ was gearing up for the Nabisco promotion Straight Arrow and Kemper, along with Tom Hanley, were scheduled to handle sound effects for the show. After doing several shows the executive producer J. Neil Reagan offered Kemper a position as writer/director with McCann-Erickson, the ad agency commissioned with the Nabisco account. He continued with the Straight Arrow show as assistant director. His desire to act led him to resign from McCann-Erickson after about a year and a half to pursue his dreams of opening doors to the celluloid world and prosperity. Kemper, now married to Novice (1945) and with a family, found his return to acting "spooky" as he had only one movie and a few radio show credits at year's end. "When an opening at CBS became available in sound effects, I took it!" For eight years Kemper produced sound effects at CBS/ KNX for some of the most popular shows in radio. In 1960 he moved to CBS Television, where he spent the remainder of his professional career as a sound mixer until retirement in 1980. Here again he worked on some of the most popular shows of the time and was nominated for an Emmy for his work with Brigadoon.

Kemper has fond memories of Straight Arrow, especially his meeting Ted Robertson, producer and director of Straight Arrow, and their eventual friendship. "Ted always publicly acknowledged me as co-producer of Straight Arrow." Kemper recalled that during the two years that he worked the show the actors and actresses worked together to create the smoothness which went to make Straight Arrow such a popular and remembered show.

Ray Kemper makes his home in the Sierra Nevada mountains with his lovely wife Novice, with whom he has celebrated over 60 years of marriage.

# Straight Arrow Radio Log

Howard Culver (R) facing Fred Howard (L) over a RCA 448X microphone. In the booth (right to left) are Ted Robertson, Ray Kemper and Lee Bolen (sitting in for regular soundman, Dick Burton)

NN    Audition script finished, January 5, 1948 - Audition New York

## DON LEE NETWORK - 1948

Thursday, 8 - 8:30 PM

Main Character Cast:
| | |
|---|---|
| Steve Adams/Straight Arrow | Howard Culver |
| Packy McCloud | Fred Howard (Wright) |
| Mesquite Molly | Gwen Delano |
| Announcer/Narrator | Frank Bingman |

1.     May 6, 1948      Stage From Calvaydos
    Cast:
    Steve Adams/Straight Arrow      Howard Culver
    Packy McCloud      Fred Howard
    Randy Culver      Harry Bartell
    Murdock      Leo Cleary
    Lacey      Joe Granby
    Mrs. Culver      Marion Richman
    Sheriff      Joe DuVal
    Voice (double)

2.     May 13, 1948      Trouble On The Trail
    Cast:
    Steve Adams/Straight Arrow      Howard Culver
    Packy McCloud      Fred Howard
    Lee Parker      Ralph Moody
    Jud Seakins      Ken Christy
    Luke Hazzard      Hal K. Dawson
    Voices

3.     May 20, 1948      False Friend
    Cast:
    Steve Adams/Straight Arrow      Howard Culver
    Packy McCloud      Fred Howard
    Carruthers      Griff Barnett
    Captain Baker      Ken Harvey
    Orderly (Lt. Sutter)      Davis Butler
    Running Antelope      Stan Waxman

4.     May 27, 1948      The Dead Man Speaks
    Cast:
    Steve Adams/Straight Arrow      Howard Culver
    Packy McCloud      Fred Howard
    Mesquite Molly      Gwen Delano
    Nancy Larrabee      Laurette Filbrandt
    Wade Larrabee      Tom Holland
    Brodell      Stanley Farrar
    Lawson      Ken Christy
    Henshaw      Jim Nusser
    Doc Witherspoon      Parley Baer
    Sheriff Tatum      Jim DuVal

5. June 3, 1948 Three On A Claim
   Cast:
   Steve Adams/Straight Arrow   Howard Culver
   Packy McCloud                Fred Howard
   Mesquite Molly               Gwen Delano
   Ellen Cartwright
   Ralph Cartwright
   Rance Hurley
   Jack-Knife Simmons

6. June 10, 1948 Wild Horse Mesa
   Cast:
   Steve Adams/Straight Arrow   Howard Culver
   Packy McCloud                Fred Howard
   Mesquite Molly               Gwen Delano
   Ralph Kincaid
   Jeff Kincaid (12 year old son)
   Link Rogers
   Shorty
   Savanah

7. June 17, 1948 Ride For Justice
   Cast:
   Steve Adams/Straight Arrow   Howard Culver
   Packy McCloud                Fred Howard
   Mesquite Molly               Gwen Delano
   Bill Crawford
   Nancy Travis
   Sheriff Taylor
   Slaughter
   Burnham
   Voice (man)

8. June 24, 1948 Pioneer Editor
   Cast:
   Steve Adams/Straight Arrow   Howard Culver
   Packy McCloud                Fred Howard
   Brett Carson
   Deborah Carson (daughter)
   Manuel Fordaz
   Deuce Morley
   Rufus Jepso
   Sheriff Naylin
   Doctor

9.     July 1, 1948     The Haunted Desert
Cast:
Steve Adams/Straight Arrow     Howard Culver
Packy McCloud     Fred Howard
Brad Foster
Jane Daley
Jarvis
Brazos
Voices (Henderson, Kelsoe, Etc)
Voice (woman)

10.     July 8, 1948     War On The Range
Cast:
Steve Adams/Straight Arrow     Howard Culver
Packy McCloud     Fred Howard
Mesquite Molly     Gwen Delano
Rufe Slaughter
Judge Harvey Watterson
Hardy Simmons
Jed Crockett
Slade
Denver

11.     July 15, 1948     Oasis In The Desert
Cast:
Steve Adams/Straight Arrow     Howard Culver
Packy McCloud     Fred Howard
Henry Dobson
Deborah Dobson
Spur Galloway
Kelsey
Ma Brady
Sheriff
Bartender (Shorty)
Voices

12.     July 22, 1948     The Iron Horse[1]
Cast:
Steve Adams/Straight Arrow     Howard Culver
Packy McCloud     Fred Howard
Mesquite Molly     Gwen Delano
Col John Frazee     Herb Butterfield
Jubal     Jim Nusser
Lockhart     Franklin Parker
Macy     Davis Butler
Ken Frazee     Rolland Morris
Voice (3)     Jim Nussar
Voice (7)     Davis Butler

13. July 29, 1948                    Danger Rides The Wind
    Cast:
    Steve Adams/Straight Arrow       Howard Culver
    Packy McCloud                    Fred Howard
    Mesquite Molly                   Gwen Delano
    Abbey Perkins
    Dale Sligby
    Ben Shortell
    Layden
    Voices

14. August 5, 1948                   Fears Saddles A Samson
    Cast:
    Steve Adams/Straight Arrow       Howard Culver
    Packy McCloud                    Fred Howard
    Mesquite Molly                   Gwen Delano
    Ben Armstrong                    Parley Baer
    Sally Armstrong                  D J Thompson
    Will Dobie                       Luis Van Rooten
    Lou                              Jack Petruzzi
    U.S. Marshall                    Bill Green
    Clawson                          Leo Curley

15. August 12, 1948                  The Gambler Holds The Cards
    Cast:
    Steve Adams/Straight Arrow       Howard Culver
    Packy McCloud                    Fred Howard
    Frenchy Orlean                   Gerry Mohr
    Josh Raven                       Herb Butterfield
    Bart Raven                       Tom Holland
    Lucy Raven                       Jane Webb
    Spike                            Dave Ellis
    Schilling                        Herb Butterfield

16. August 19, 1948                  Double For Danger
    Cast:
    Steve Adams/Straight Arrow       Howard Culver
    Packy McCloud                    Fred Howard
    Mesquite Molly                   Gwen Delano
    Dade Gleason                     Parley Baer
    Silk Selden                      Willard Waterman
    Luke                             Jack Petruzzi
    Dirk                             Tony Barrett
    Mr. Gerrold                      Cy Kendall
    Doctor                           Parley Baer
    Voice (woman)                    Lillian Buyeff

17.  August 26, 1948              Badmen Cross The Bravo
     Cast:
     Steve Adams/Straight Arrow   Howard Culver
     Packy McCloud                Fred Howard
     Manuel Fordaz                Nestor Paiva
     Mina Fordaz                  Peggy Webber
     Ysidro Fordaz                Jay Novello
     Hardin                       Ken Christy
     Killeen                      Jay Novello
     Sheriff Wylie                Rolf Sedan
     Voices (men)

18.  September 2, 1948            The Ringer
     Cast:
     Steve Adams/Straight Arrow   Howard Culver
     Packy McCloud                Fred Howard
     Mesquite Molly               Gwen Delano
     Col Wynstandley              Parley Baer
     Jim Wynstandley              David Ellis
     Major Parker                 Earle Ross
     Sally Parker                 Marian Richman
     Jake Morley                  Bill Bouchey
     Skillman                     Wilms Herbert
     Man                          Wilms Herbert

19.  September 9, 1948            The Redman Traps A Killer
     Cast:
     Steve Adams/Straight Arrow   Howard Culver
     Packy McCloud                Fred Howard
     Jacknife                     Ed MacDonald
     Spike Selby                  Jack Kruschen
     Frenchy Beauchamp            Ken Harvey
     Graw Murtrie                 Charlie Lung
     Colonel                      Stan Waxman
     Brace                        Charlie Seel
     Orderly (double)             Jack Kruschen

20.  September 16, 1948           Flame And Fury
     Cast:
     Steve Adams/Straight Arrow   Howard Culver
     Packy McCloud                Fred Howard
     Mesquite Molly               Gwen Delano
     Hardy Kenwood                Tim Graham
     Sarah Kenwood                Ruth Rickaby
     Will Franklin                Stan Farrar
     Ringo (~~double~~)           Ken Christy

|     |                                    |                    |
| --- | ---------------------------------- | ------------------ |
|     | Hannah Franklin                    | Rena Craig         |
|     | Sheriff                            | Joe DuVal          |
|     | Man (double)                       | Joe DuVal          |
|     | Woman (double)                     | Rena Craig         |
| 21. | September 23, 1948                 | Spanish Gold       |
|     | Cast:                              |                    |
|     | Steve Adams/Straight Arrow         | Howard Culver      |
|     | Packy McCloud                      | Fred Howard        |
|     | Mesquite Molly                     | Gwen Delano        |
|     | Jeff Williams                      | Harry Bartell      |
|     | Lucy Williams                      | Virginia Gregg     |
|     | Rafe Smiley                        | Luis Van Rooten    |
|     | Wade Travis                        | Wilms Herbert      |
| 22. | September 30, 1948                 | Ambush At Eagle Pass |
|     | Cast:                              |                    |
|     | Steve Adams/Straight Arrow         | Howard Culver      |
|     | Packy McCloud                      | Fred Howard        |
|     | Slade                              | Jack Petruzzi      |
|     | Huggins                            | Earl Lee           |
|     | Stagecoach Driver                  | Ralph Moody        |
|     | Dirkson                            | Jeff Corey         |
|     | Murdock                            | David Ellis        |
|     | Henry Butterfield                  | Parley Baer        |
|     | Kelland                            | Earl Lee           |
|     | Driver                             | Ralph Moody        |
| 23. | October 7, 1948                    | The Hero           |
|     | Cast:                              |                    |
|     | Steve Adams/Straight Arrow         | Howard Culver      |
|     | Packy McCloud                      | Fred Howard        |
|     | Mesquite Molly                     | Gwen Delano        |
|     | Bart                               | Joe DuVal          |
|     | Ramsey                             | Jess Kirkpatrick   |
|     | Professor                          | Parley Baer        |
|     | Slash                              | Wilms Herbert      |
|     | Lafe                               | Harry Lang         |
|     | Women (double)                     | Florence Wolcott   |

24. October 14, 1948     Cry Of The Wolf
Cast:
| | |
|---|---|
| Steve Adams/Straight Arrow | Howard Culver |
| Packy McCloud | Fred Howard |
| Harvey Forrester | Jack Edwards |
| Pike | Dave Ellis |
| Dutch | Jack Kruschen |
| Sheriff | Joe DuVal |
| Wolf | Harry Lang |
| Voice | Malcolm McCoy |
| Voice #2 | Harry Lang |

25. October 21, 1948     Pony Express
Cast:
| | |
|---|---|
| Steve Adams/Straight Arrow | Howard Culver |
| Packy McCloud | Fred Howard |
| Mesquite Molly | Gwen Delano |
| Davey Cartwright | Jerry Farber |
| Mother Cartwright | Rena Craig |
| Mr. Bailey | Ken Christy |
| Trigger | Jim Arvin |
| Dallas | Tim Graham |
| Postmaster | Earl Lee |
| Voice | Earl Lee |
| Voice #2 | John T. Smith |

26. October 28, 1948     Trailblazer
Cast:
| | |
|---|---|
| Steve Adams/Straight Arrow | Howard Culver |
| Packy McCloud | Fred Howard |
| Mesquite Molly | Gwen Delano |
| Lije Jefferson | Bill Lally |
| Lucy Jefferson | Lillian Buyeff |
| Crunch | Luis Van Rooten |
| Dallas | Jack Petruzzi |
| Cantrell | Jess Kirkpatrick |
| Doc (double) | Stan Waxman |
| Voice | Stan Waxman |

27. November 4, 1948     Rainbow's End
Cast:
| | |
|---|---|
| Steve Adams/Straight Arrow | Howard Culver |
| Packy McCloud | Fred Howard |
| Ethan Daniels | Leonard Smith |
| Mother Daniels | Lisa Morgan |
| Bracken | Charley McGraw |
| Quirt | David Ellis |
| Judge Prentice | Stan Farrar |
| Voice | Paul Dubov |

| | | |
|---|---|---|
| 28. | November 11, 1948 | The Sheriff (Wins) Earns His Spurs |
| | Cast: | |
| | Steve Adams/Straight Arrow | Howard Culver |
| | Packy McCloud | Fred Howard |
| | Mesquite Molly | Gwen Delano |
| | Sheriff Frazer | Ken Peters |
| | Ruth Frazer | Ann Diamond |
| | Deputy Bickworth | Tyler McVey |
| | Mayor Peabody | Bill Green(e) |
| | Red Dawson | Bill Bouchey |
| | Killik | Eddie Fields |
| | Voice | Herb Vigran |
| 29. | November 18, 1948 | The Boomer |
| | Cast: | |
| | Steve Adams/Straight Arrow | Howard Culver |
| | Packy McCloud | Fred Howard |
| | Gregor Duncan | Jack Lewis |
| | Mary Duncan | Mary Gordon |
| | Tack | Ralph Moody |
| | Slaughter | Charlie Lung |
| | Voices (Lance Honeycutt, etc) | Parley Baer |
| 30. | November 25, 1948 | The Wild Turkey |
| | Cast: | |
| | Steve Adams/Straight Arrow | Howard Culver |
| | Packy McCloud | Fred Howard |
| | Pietro Con Vaya | Nestor Paiva |
| | Senora Con Vaya | Lillian Buyeff |
| | Roberta | Harry Bartell |
| | Dillon | Ken Christy |
| | Jarvis | Ralph Moody |
| | Shorty | Vic Perrin |
| | Sheriff | Joe DuVal |
| | Judge | Earl Lee |

....PIN ALL THE STOLEN CATTLE ON ROBERTO....

Sketch by Frank Bingman.

31.  December 2, 1948                The Turncoat
     Cast:
     Steve Adams/Straight Arrow      Howard Culver
     Packy McCloud                   Fred Howard
     Mesquite Molly                  Gwen Delano
     Private Scott Lacey             Rolland Morris
     Sergeant Mulroy                 Jack Lewis
     Captain Ramrod Flint            Earle Ross
     Dirk                            Jack Petruzzi
     Skillman                        Wilms Herbert

32.  December 9, 1948                Bounty Hunter
     Cast:
     Steve Adams/Straight Arrow      Howard Culver
     Packy McCloud                   Fred Howard
     Miles Tandee                    Eddie Firestone
     Chad Dennison                   Parley Baer
     Lisbeth Dennison                Jane Webb
     Armand Charcot                  Wilms Herbert

33.  December 16, 1948               Doctor And The Quack
     Cast:
     Steve Adams/Straight Arrow      Howard Culver
     Packy McCloud                   Fred Howard
     Mesquite Molly                  Gwen Delano
     Doc Begley                      Earl Lee
     Turk                            Jack Kruschen
     Brad Collins                    Ken Peters
     Miss Sarah Vesey                Marian Richman
     Sheriff Tate                    Joe DuVal
     Voice (man)                     Jack Kruschen

34.  December 23, 1948               Sheep (For) In The Manger
     Cast:
     Steve Adams/Straight Arrow      Howard Culver
     Packy McCloud                   Fred Howard
     Wyatt Blakey (8 years)          Jeffrey Silver
     Ma Blakley                      Virginia Gregg
     Bob Blakely (Pa)                Barton Yarborough
     Mister Talbot                   John Dehner
     Man                             Jan Arvin
     Man #2                          John Dehner

35.     December 30, 1948              The Long Trail
        Cast:
        Steve Adams/Straight Arrow      Howard Culver
        Packy McCloud                   Fred Howard
        Mesquite Molly                  Gwen Delano
        Sheriff Hawkins                 Tyler McVey
        Tate                            Herb Butterfield
        Bowie                           Jack Edwards
        Link                            Luis Van Rotten
        Man (Matt, etc)                 Jack Petruzzi
        Deputy                          Herb Butterfield

## DON LEE NETWORK - 1949

36.     January 6, 1949                 Rolling Wheels
        Cast:
        Steve Adams/Straight Arrow      Howard Culver
        Packy McCloud                   Fred Howard
        Agent Davis                     Charley Lung
        Slaughter                       Ed Max
        Cain                            Don Diamond
        Sheriff                         Joe DuVal
        Montana (double)                Harry Bartell
        Wash Huckins                    Harry Bartell
        Deborah                         Ann Diamond
        Man (double)                    Don Diamond
        Woman (double)                  Ann Diamond

37.     January 13, 1949                The Widow's Might
        Cast:
        Steve Adams/Straight Arrow      Howard Culver
        Packy McCloud                   Fred Howard
        Bashful                         Malcolm McCoy
        Masters                         Ken Christy
        Amanda                          Constance Crowder
        Curran                          Harry Lang
        Man                             Joe DuVal
        Strong                          Tim Graham
        Sheriff                         Joe DuVal

38. January 20, 1949 — The High Mountain
    Cast:
    Steve Adams/Straight Arrow — Howard Culver
    Packy McCloud — Fred Howard
    Sven Pederson — Ken Peters
    Cuttybone — Herb Vigran
    Lije — Charlie Seel
    Man (double) — Parley Baer
    Dr. Hawthorne — Parley Baer

39. January 27, 1949 — Cattle Train [2]
    Cast:
    Steve Adams/Straight Arrow — Howard Culver
    Packy McCloud — Fred Howard
    Ace Henshaw — Jack McIntyre
    Dirk — Jack Kruschen
    Bartender (double) — Franklin Parker
    Passenger (double) — Franklin Parker
    Engineer — Grey Stafford

## MUTUAL BROADCASTING SYSTEM - 1949

Mondays, 8 - 8:30 PM
Tuesday, 5 - 5:30 PM
Thursday, 5 - 5:30 PM

40. February 7, 1949, Monday — The Roaring River [3]
    Cast:
    Steve Adams/Straight Arrow — Howard Culver
    Packy McCloud — Fred Howard
    Mesquite Molly — Gwen Delano
    Capt Josh Crayley — Parley Baer
    Snake — Luis Van Rooten
    Bart — Jack Petruzzi
    Agent (double) — Joe DuVal
    Sheriff (double Agent) — Joe DuVal

41. February 8, 1949, Tuesday — The Hermit of Crosshollow Ridge
    Cast:
    Steve Adams/Straight Arrow — Howard Culver
    Packy McCloud — Fred Howard
    Jed Parker — Ralph Moody
    Lance Parker — Wilms Herbert
    Sheriff — Herb Butterfield
    Idaho — Nestor Paiva

| | | |
|---|---|---|
| 42. | February 10, 1949, Thursday | Buffalo Hunt [4] |
| | Cast: | |
| | Steve Adams/Straight Arrow | Howard Culver |
| | Packy McCloud | Fred Howard |
| | Sheriff Brainard | Bob Holton |
| | Ned Brainard | Sam Edwards |
| | Jackdaw Simmons | Jess Kirkpatrick |
| 43. | February 14, 1949, Monday | Grubstake |
| | Cast: | |
| | Steve Adams/Straight Arrow | Howard Culver |
| | Packy McCloud | Fred Howard |
| | Mesquite Molly | Gwen Delano |
| | Jonathan Peabody | Tim Graham |
| | Eldorado Brink | Clarence Hartzell |
| | Bartender | Lou Krugman |
| | Ephram Simmons | John Dehner |
| | Woman (double) | Gwen Delano |
| 44. | February 15, 1949, Tuesday | Pioneer Crossing |
| | Cast: | |
| | Steve Adams/Straight Arrow | Howard Culver |
| | Packy McCloud | Fred Howard |
| | Clem Burdock | Parley Baer |
| | Hardy | Eddie Firestone |
| | Spider | Paul Conrad |
| | Nevada | Tyler McVey |
| | Marshall | Charles Seel |
| | Doctor | Parley Baer |
| | Driver | Jim Nusser |
| 45. | February 17, 1949, Thursday | Ambush In The Desert |
| | Cast: | |
| | Steve Adams/Straight Arrow | Howard Culver |
| | Packy McCloud | Fred Howard |
| | Mesquite Molly | Gwen Delano |
| | Scar | Ed Max |
| | Rawhide | Jack Petruzzi |
| | Guide | Herb Butterfield |
| | Tad | Bobby Ellis |
| | Woman | Rena Craig |
| | Man | Jack Petruzzi |
| | Man 2 | Herb Butterfield |

46. February 21, 1949, Monday — Stampede For Justice
Cast:
|  |  |
|---|---|
| Steve Adams/Straight Arrow | Howard Culver |
| Packy McCloud | Fred Howard |
| Abby Kimbrough | Ann Diamond |
| Andrew Kimbrough | Whitfield Connor |
| Montana | Vic Perrin |
| Bragg | Ken Christy |
| Man 1 | Earl Lee |
| Sheriff | Joe DuVal |

47. February 22, 1949, Tuesday — Ride The Twister
Cast:
|  |  |
|---|---|
| Steve Adams/Straight Arrow | Howard Culver |
| Packy McCloud | Fred Howard |
| Blackie | John Dehner |
| Rickey | Jeffrey Silver |
| Alex | Jack Lewis |
| Kelsoe | Frank Gerstle |
| Shorty | Jan Arvin |

48. February 24, 1949, Thursday — Mark Of The Coward
Cast:
|  |  |
|---|---|
| Steve Adams/Straight Arrow | Howard Culver |
| Packy McCloud | Fred Howard |
| Torrent | Lou Merrill |
| Voice | Charlie Lung |
| Man | Jack Petruzzi |
| Loftus | Ken Peters |
| Murtrie | Charlie Lung |
| Weasel | Jack Petruzzi |
| Nancy | Virginia Gregg |
| Jarvis | Charles Seel |

49. February 28, 1949, Monday — Rainbow Canyon
Cast: No information available

50. March 1, 1949, Tuesday — Log Jam
Cast: No information available

51. March 3, 1949, Thursday — Badlands Hideout
Cast:
|  |  |
|---|---|
| Steve Adams/Straight Arrow | Howard Culver |
| Packy McCloud | Fred Howard |
| Ringo | Marc Lawrence |
| Will | Eric Lord |

|  |  |  |
|---|---|---|
|  | Lawson | Charlie Seel |
|  | Man (double) | Wilms Herbert |
|  | Scabbard | Wilms Herbert |
| 52. | March 7, 1949, Monday | Homestead Hunger |
|  | Cast: |  |
|  | Steve Adams/Straight Arrow | Howard Culver |
|  | Packy McCloud | Fred Howard |
|  | Mesquite Molly | Gwen Delano |
|  | Ned Sayer | Whitfield Conner |
|  | Ruth Sayer | Kay Stewart |
|  | Korcy | Earle Ross |
|  | Gopher | John Dehner |
| 53. | March 8, 1949, Tuesday | Cattle Baron |
|  | Cast: |  |
|  | Steve Adams/Straight Arrow | Howard Culver |
|  | Packy McCloud | Fred Howard |
|  | Sean O'Brien | Tim Graham |
|  | Blaine Doxey | Nestor Paiva |
|  | Denver | Jack Petruzzi |
|  | Sheever | Edward Van Sloan |
|  | Man (double) |  |
|  | Sheriff | Ralph Moody |
| 54. | March 10, 1949, Thursday | The Wager |
|  | Cast: |  |
|  | Steve Adams/Straight Arrow | Howard Culver |
|  | Packy McCloud | Fred Howard |
|  | Murtrie McGregor | Jack Lewis |
|  | Jaques Laport | Jan Arvin |
|  | Fargo | Bill Bouchey |
|  | Duroc | Barney Phillips |
| 55. | March 14, 1949, Monday | (Red Feather Headband) |
|  | Cast: | Band Of The Red Feather |
|  | Steve Adams/Straight Arrow | Howard Culver |
|  | Packy McCloud | Fred Howard |
|  | Running Bison | Wilms Herbert |
|  | Corporal (double) | Wilms Herbert |
|  | Man (double) | Stan Waxman |
|  | Colonel Devering | Earle Ross |
|  | Lucy Devering | Jeanne Bates |
|  | Sutter | Ken Christy |
|  | Lt Larry Masters | Whitfield Connor |
|  | Voice (double) | Fred Howard |
|  | Captain | Stan Waxman |

56.     March 15, 1949, Tuesday          Redman's Rescue
        Cast:
        Steve Adams/Straight Arrow        Howard Culver
        Packy McCloud                     Fred Howard
        Mesquite Molly                    Gwen Delano
        Grey Eagle                        Ralph Moody
        Kenesaw                           Edward Van Sloan
        Slaughter                         Parley Baer
        Shag                              Jack Petruzzi
        Sheriff                           Tim Graham

57.     March 17, 1949, Thursday         Badge Of Courage
        Cast: No information available

58.     March 21, 1949, Monday           Badmen Unmasked (55)
        Cast:
        Steve Adams/Straight Arrow        Howard Culver
        Packy McCloud                     Fred Howard
        Mesquite Molly                    Gwen Delano
        Dale Gleason                      Bud Widom
        Martha Gleason                    Connie Crowder
        Murchison                         Lou Merrill
        Slagle                            Bob Strange
        Chandler                          Charlie Seel
        Man (double)                      Charlie Seel
        Man 2 (double)                    Bob Strange

59.     March 22, 1949, Tuesday          The Blue Clay (56)
        Cast:
        Steve Adams/Straight Arrow        Howard Culver
        Packy McCloud                     Fred Howard
        Tom Gillespie                     Dick Anderson
        Jed Lockwood                      Ralph Moody
        Flint                             Nestor Paiva
        Denver                            Jack Petruzzi
        Doctor Lacey                      Malcolm McCoy

60.     March 24, 1949, Thursday         Land Of Our Fathers (57) [5]
        Cast:
        Steve Adams/Straight Arrow        Howard Culver
        Packy McCloud                     Fred Howard
        Monty                             Ken Christy
        Spur                              Tyler McVey
        Judge Prentice                    Ted von Eltz
        White Cloud                       Bill Green
        Brave                             Barney Phillips
        Man (double)                      Barney Phillips

61. March 28, 1949, Monday     Friend In Need
    Cast:
    Steve Adams/Straight Arrow     Howard Culver
    Packy McCloud     Fred Howard
    Mesquite Molly     Gwen Delano
    Bobby Weatherby     Jeff Silver
    Peter Weatherby     Barton Yarborough
    Norah Weatherby     Vivi Janiss
    Jackal     Jack Kruschen
    Lash     Vic Perrin

62. March 29, 1949, Tuesday     Relay Station
    Cast:
    Steve Adams/Straight Arrow     Howard Culver
    Packy McCloud     Fred Howard
    Nokotani     Jan Arvin
    Link     Jack Petruzzi
    Bracken     Ken Christy
    Indian (double)     Parley Baer
    Peabody     Ben Wright
    Driver     Parley Baer

63. March 31, 1949, Thursday     Terror Township
    Cast:
    Steve Adams/Straight Arrow     Howard Culver
    Packy McCloud     Fred Howard
    Washoe     Lou Merrill
    Denver     Jack Edwards
    Parker     Harry Bartell
    Abby     Virginia Gregg
    Man (double)     Earl Lee Huntington
    Man 2 (double)     Earl Lee Huntington

64. April 4, 1949, Monday     His Honor, The Mayor
    Cast:
    Steve Adams/Straight Arrow     Howard Culver
    Packy McCloud     Fred Howard
    Mesquite Molly     Gwen Delano
    Lex Gurney     John Dehner
    King Murdock     Bill Bouchey
    Trigger     Paul Conrad
    Man     Malcolm McCoy
    Man 2     Hal Dawson

| | | |
|---|---|---|
| 65. | April 5, 1949, Tuesday | Rustlers' Gap |
| | Cast: | |
| | Steve Adams/Straight Arrow | Howard Culver |
| | Packy McCloud | Fred Howard |
| | Flint | Willard Waterman |
| | Bradon | Jack Petruzzi |
| | Slick | Bill Justine |
| | Sheriff | Parley Baer |
| | Man | Jack Petruzzi |
| 66. | April 7, 1949, Thursday | Pueblo Of The Sky |
| | Cast: | |
| | Steve Adams/Straight Arrow | Howard Culver |
| | Packy McCloud | Fred Howard |
| | Sakadari | Ralph Moody |
| | Lance | Ken Christy |
| | Bull | Jack Kruschen |
| | Chief | Bill Green |
| 67. | April 11, 1949, Monday | Brand Of The Badmen |
| | Cast: | |
| | Steve Adams/Straight Arrow | Howard Culver |
| | Packy McCloud | Fred Howard |
| | Warcloud | Jan Arvin |
| | Rogers | Charles Seel |
| | Trig | Jack Petruzzi |
| | Bolo | Nestor Paiva |
| | Sheriff | Tudor Owen |
| | Man (double) | Joe Forte |
| 68. | April 12, 1949, Tuesday | The Lawless Land |
| | Cast: | |
| | Steve Adams/Straight Arrow | Howard Culver |
| | Packy McCloud | Fred Howard |
| | Cartwright | Steve Dunne |
| | Smokey | Jack Kruschen |
| | Man (double) | Jack Edwards |
| | King Brainard | Lou Merrill |
| | Hendricks | Parley Baer |
| | Man 2 (double) | Parley Baer |
| | Man 3 (double) | Jack Edwards |
| | Man 4 (double) | Jack Kruschen |

69. April 11, 1949, Thursday — Double Danger
Cast:
Steve Adams/Straight Arrow — Howard Culver
Packy McCloud — Fred Howard
Stefani Martin — Anne Diamond
Jack Reardon — Earle Ross
Lance Murdock — Ken Christy
Shorty — Pinky Parker

70. April 18, 1949, Monday — The Golden Flood
Cast:
Steve Adams/Straight Arrow — Howard Culver
Packy McCloud — Fred Howard
Scragg — Ed Max
Crabtree — Willard Waterman
Wakuta — Michael Chapin
Chief — Ralph Moody
Sheriff Barker — Joe DuVal

71. April 19, 1949, Tuesday — Border Justice
Cast:
Steve Adams/Straight Arrow — Howard Culver
Packy McCloud — Fred Howard
Lt Bradwell — Whitfield Connor
Captain (double) — Parley Baer
Saber — Jack Petruzzi
Larrabee — Lou Merrill
Sheriff Hardy — Tim Graham
Doc (double) — Parley Baer
Denver — Jan Arvin
Man (double) — Fred Howard

72. April 21, 1949, Thursday — The Peddler Of Pecos
Cast:
Steve Adams/Straight Arrow — Howard Culver
Packy McCloud — Fred Howard
Sam Puddleby — Junius Matthews
Travis — Ken Christy
Link — Nestor Paiva
Man (double) — Charlie Seel
Sheriff Carter — Charlie Seel

73.  April 25, 1949, Monday         Justice Beats The Law
     Cast:
     Steve Adams/Straight Arrow     Howard Culver
     Packy McCloud                  Fred Howard
     Bearclaw                       John Dehner
     Crooked Snake                  Wilms Herbert
     Slaughter                      Lou Merrill
     Curly                          Marc Lawrence
     Marshall                       Ben Wright
     Running Bison                  Ben Wright

74.  April 26, 1949, Tuesday        False Trail
     Cast:
     Steve Adams/Straight Arrow     Howard Culver
     Packy McCloud                  Fred Howard
     Williams                       Barney Phillips
     Denning                        Parley Baer
     Hazen                          Ken Christy
     Dirk                           Jack Petruzzi
     Man (double)                   Vic Perrin

75.  April 28, 1949, Thursday       Thicker Than Water
     Cast:
     Steve Adams/Straight Arrow     Howard Culver
     Packy McCloud                  Fred Howard
     Luke Badger                    Steve Dunne
     Jim Badger                     Dick Crenna
     Slade                          Ed May
     Sheriff                        Charlie Seel
     Deputy                         Tim Graham

76.  May 2, 1949, Monday            Thunder Gorge
     Cast:
     Steve Adams/Straight Arrow     Howard Culver
     Packy McCloud                  Fred Howard
     Abby Chadwick                  Kay Stewart
     Dave Chadwick                  Whit Connor
     Burley                         Earl Ross
     Denver                         Jack Petruzzi
     Washoe                         Harry Lang
     Lacey                          Charlie Lung
     Sheriff                        Charlie Lung

77. May 3, 1949, Tuesday           The Shaggy River
    Cast:
    Steve Adams/Straight Arrow     Howard Culver
    Packy McCloud                  Fred Howard
    Lightfoot                      Jan Arvin
    Smedley                        Lou Merrill
    Lynch                          Bill Bouchey
    Doctor                         Parley Baer
    Man (double)                   Jan Arvin
    Dakota-Running Bear            Ralph Moody
    Sheriff                        Ralph Moody

78. May 5, 1949, Thursday          Stage For El Paso
    Cast:
    Steve Adams/Straight Arrow     Howard Culver
    Packy McCloud                  Fred Howard
    Rocky                          Ken Christy
    Vegas                          Nestor Paiva
    Sheriff                        Hal Dawson
    Bar                            Jan Arvin
    Lightfoot                      Jan Arvin
    Laramie                        Tim Graham

79. May 9, 1949, Monday            Remounts
    Cast:
    Steve Adams/Straight Arrow     Howard Culver
    Packy McCloud                  Fred Howard
    Aiken                          Bill Bouchey
    Lt Nelson                      Ken Peters
    Piegan                         John Dehner
    Spur                           Vic Perrin
    Antler                         Dick Crenna
    Man (double)                   John Dehner

80. May 10, 1949, Tuesday          Smoke And (Flame) Fire
    Cast:
    Steve Adams/Straight Arrow     Howard Culver
    Packy McCloud                  Fred Howard
    Sheriff                        Parley Baer
    Weasel                         Jack Petruzzi
    Spur                           Wilms Herbert
    Rawden                         Ken Christy
    Crook (double)                 Malcolm McCoy
    Man (double)                   Wilms Herbert
    Storekeeper                    Malcolm McCoy

81. May 12, 1949, Thursday     False Partner
    Cast:
    Steve Adams/Straight Arrow     Howard Culver
    Packy McCloud     Fred Howard
    Williams     Whit Connor
    Blakey     Harry Bartell
    Sneed     Lou Merrill
    Craven     Tyler McVey
    Sheriff     Jess Kirkpatrick
    Man (double)     Fred Howard

82. May 16, 1949, Monday     Drumbeat
    Cast:
    Steve Adams/Straight Arrow     Howard Culver
    Packy McCloud     Fred Howard
    Colonel Henshaw     Ted von Eltz
    Lightfoot     Jan Arvin
    Crooked Wing     Wilms Herbert
    Lynch     Nestor Paiva
    Craven     Ken Christy
    Running Deer     Ralph Moody
    Corporal (double)     Jan Arvin
    Indian (double)     Nestor Paiva

83. May 17, 1949, Tuesday     Call To Valor
    Cast:
    Steve Adams/Straight Arrow     Howard Culver
    Packy McCloud     Fred Howard
    Morlake     Lou Merrill
    Scar     Jack Petruzzi
    Carson     Parley Baer
    Sheriff     Tim Graham
    Man (double)     Tim Graham

84. May 19, 1949, Thursday     The Quaking Bush
    Cast:
    Steve Adams/Straight Arrow     Howard Culver
    Packy McCloud     Fred Howard
    Sheriff     Charlie Seel
    Bates     J(?). Sheldon
    Dobie     Jack Kruschen
    Flash     Bill Bouchey
    Montana     Eddie Fields

85. May 23, 1949, Monday          Desert Telegraph
    Cast:
    Steve Adams/Straight Arrow    Howard Culver
    Packy McCloud                 Fred Howard
    Wolf                          Lou Merrill
    Shanty                        Pinky Parker
    Cooper                        Junius Matthews
    Captain                       Stan Waxman
    Lieutenant                    Grey Stafford

86. May 24, 1949, Tuesday         Flash Flood
    Cast:
    Steve Adams/Straight Arrow    Howard Culver
    Packy McCloud                 Fred Howard
    Brand                         Bill Bouchey
    Rawhide                       Jack Petruzzi
    Raven                         Ralph Moody
    Greyling                      Wilms Herbert
    Indian (double)               Jim Nusser
    Man (double)                  Jim Nusser

87. May 26, 1949, Thursday        Blood Brothers
    Cast:
    Steve Adams/Straight Arrow    Howard Culver
    Packy McCloud                 Fred Howard
    Sheriff Lawson                Charlie Seel
    Buck Carson                   Nestor Pavia
    Snake                         Paul Conrad
    Shawnee                       Vic Perrin
    Wadota                        Richard Crenna
    Shallick                      Charlie Lung
    Man (double)                  Richard Crenna
    Judge (double)                Charlie Lung

88. May 30, 1949, Monday          Reluctant Witness
    Cast:
    Steve Adams/Straight Arrow    Howard Culver
    Packy McCloud                 Fred Howard
    Chad Rountree                 Ken Peters
    Sheriff Granger               Tim Graham
    Dave Torrent                  Lou Merrill
    Scragg                        Nestor Pavia
    Lightfoot                     Jan Arvin
    Man                           Barney Phillips

89. May 31, 1949, Tuesday          News Beats The Drum
    Cast:
    Steve Adams/Straight Arrow     Howard Culver
    Packy McCloud                  Fred Howard
    Angus McGregor                 Tudor Owen
    Stone                          Ken Christy
    Brace                          Jack Petruzzi
    Lije Hendricks                 Earl Lee Huntington
    Sheriff                        Ralph Moody
    Indian (double)                Ralph Moody

90. June 2, 1949, Thursday         Raiding Party
    Cast:
    Steve Adams/Straight Arrow     Howard Culver
    Packy McCloud                  Fred Howard
    Lt Foster                      Whit Connor
    Sergeant Brady                 Charlie Seel
    Chief Lightfoot                Jan Arvin
    Colonel (double)               Ted von Eltz
    Indian (double)                Ted von Eltz
    Man (double)                   Jan Arvin
    Galloway                       William (Bill) Bouchey

91. June 6, 1949, Monday           Downgrade To Death
    Cast:
    Steve Adams/Straight Arrow     Howard Culver
    Packy McCloud                  Fred Howard
    Jeff Stanton                   Richard Crenna
    Shad Rankin                    Lou Merrill
    Trig                           Jack Petruzzi
    Deborah Stanton                Jane Webb
    Sheriff Badger                 Joe DuVal
    Station Agent (double)         Earl Lee Huntington
    Engineer (double)              Joe DuVal
    Man (double)                   Earl Lee Huntington

92. June 7, 1949, Tuesday          Fire In The Wind
    Cast:
    Steve Adams/Straight Arrow     Howard Culver
    Packy McCloud                  Fred Howard
    Running Bear                   Ralph Moody
    Sheriff                        Parley Baer
    Crimp                          Bill Bouchey
    Slavin                         Nestor Pavia

Straight Arrow Radio Log 53

93. June 9, 1949, Thursday    Bounty For Bear
Cast:
Steve Adams/Straight Arrow    Howard Culver
Packy McCloud    Fred Howard
Leveret    Charlie Seel
Man (double)    D(?). Oreck
Chicoya    Vic Perrin
Flint    Ken Christy
Slade    Wilms Herbert
Grizzly Bear    Earl Keen

94. June 13, 1949, Monday    Bridge To Calvaydos
Cast:
Steve Adams/Straight Arrow    Howard Culver
Packy McCloud    Fred Howard
Raven    Lou Merrill
Dirk    Paul Conrad
Dale Kirwood    Whit Connor
Jasper    Jack Petruzzi
Sheriff    Charlie Seel
Running Bear    Ralph Moody
Judge (double)    Charlie Seel
Marshall (double)    Ralph Moody

95. June 14, 1949, Tuesday    Signal For Danger
Cast:
Steve Adams/Straight Arrow    Howard Culver
Packy McCloud    Fred Howard
Ralph Lockwood    Richard Crenna
Jonathan Kelto    Parley Baer
Chase    Wilms Herbert
Clem Barton    Tim McVey
Scar    Jan Arvin
Sheriff    Jan Arvin

96. June 16, 1949, Thursday    Land Rush
Cast:
Steve Adams/Straight Arrow    Howard Culver
Packy McCloud    Fred Howard
Dan Procter    Barton Yarborough
Mary Procter    Connie Crowder
Nails    Jack Kruschen
Morlake    Nestor Pavia
Marshall    Tim Graham

## Mondays 8 - 8:30 PM

97.  June 20, 1949                          Comanche Trail [6]
     Cast:
     Steve Adams/Straight Arrow          Howard Culver
     Packy McCloud                       Fred Howard
     Spur                                Jack Petruzzi
     Catlin                              Nestor Paiva
     Sanders                             Steve Dunne
     Forrester                           Bill Bouchey
     Medicine Man                        Ralph Moody
     Youth                               Dick Crenna
     Man (double)                        Ralph Moody
     Man 2 (double)                      Bill Bouchey

98.  June 27, 1949                          New Leaf
     Cast:
     Steve Adams/Straight Arrow          Howard Culver
     Packy McCloud                       Fred Howard
     Shiftless Jones                     Parley Baer
     Widow Lester                        Rena Craig
     Caffee                              Lou Merrill
     Gentry                              Wilms Herbert
     Buck                                Jack Petruzzi

99.  July 4, 1949                           Free And Equal
     Cast:
     Steve Adams/Straight Arrow          Howard Culver
     Packy McCloud                       Fred Howard
     Mesquite Molly                      Gwen Delano
     Pedro Camillo                       Nestor Paiva
     Parsons                             Charlie Seel
     King Cain                           Lou Merrill
     Latigo                              Vic Perrin
     Man                                 Charlie Lung
     Woman                               Connie Crowder
     Man 2                               Charlie Lung

100. July 11, 1949                          Thunder Gap
     Cast:
     Steve Adams/Straight Arrow          Howard Culver
     Packy McCloud                       Fred Howard
     Bart Sawyer                         Ernie (?) Winstanley
     Lije Grant                          Parley Baer
     Grey Cloud                          Ralph Moody
     Barbara Grant                       Jane Webb
     Nails                               Jack Petruzzi
     Fargo                               Ken Christy

101. July 18, 1949                                Crooked Trail
     Cast:
     Steve Adams/Straight Arrow                   Howard Culver
     Packy McCloud                                Fred Howard
     Slagle                                       John Dehner
     Burley                                       Lou Merrill
     Denver                                       Jack Petruzzi
     Kincaid                                      Harry Bartell
     Granger                                      Ted von Eltz
     Williams                                     Parley Baer
     Voice (double)                               Ted von Eltz
     Voice #2 (double)                            Parley Baer

102. July 25, 1949                                Merchants Of Murder
     Cast:
     Steve Adams/Straight Arrow                   Howard Culver
     Packy McCloud                                Fred Howard
     Mesquite Molly                               Gwen Delano
     Rocky                                        Franklin Parker
     Slaughter                                    Ken Christy
     Chief Warclub                                Wilms Herbert
     Colonel                                      William (Bill) Bouchey
     Corporal (double)                            Wilms Herbert
     Cartwright                                   Tim Graham

103. August 1, 1949                               Meeting Of The Rails
     Cast:
     Steve Adams/Straight Arrow                   Howard Culver
     Packy McCloud                                Fred Howard
     Clinch                                       Lou Merrill
     Snake                                        Jack Petruzzi
     General Foster                               Parley Baer
     Wong                                         Charlie Lung
     Gallagher                                    Joe DuVal
     Voice (double)                               Jan Arvin
     Voice 2 (double)                             Jan Arvin
     Commercial                                   Jeffrey Silver

104. August 8, 1949                               The Chase
     Cast:
     Steve Adams/Straight Arrow                   Howard Culver
     Packy McCloud                                Fred Howard
     Welk                                         Vic Perrin
     Buzz                                         Ken Christy
     Penemaqua                                    Ralph Moody
     Sheriff                                      Charles Seel
     Voice (double)                               Ralph Moody
     Commercial                                   Marion Richman

105. August 15, 1949                Greed For Gold
     Cast:
     Steve Adams/Straight Arrow     Howard Culver
     Packy McCloud                  Fred Howard
     Mesquite Molly                 Gwen Delano
     Clem Bartlett                  Tim Graham
     Hop Sawyer                     Harry Bartell
     Debby                          Virginia Gregg
     Griffin                        Jack Petruzzi
     Sheriff                        Parley Baer
     Woman (double)                 Virginia Gregg
     Indian                         Jan Arvin
     Voice (double)                 Jan Arvin

106. August 22, 1949                The Renegade
     Cast:
     Steve Adams/Straight Arrow     Howard Culver
     Packy McCloud                  Fred Howard
     Trigger Slade                  Wilms Herbert
     Marshall Bates                 Earl Lee Huntington
     Spotted Fawn                   Jane Webb
     Chief Ondara                   Bill Green

107. August 29, 1949                The Last Run
     Cast:
     Steve Adams/Straight Arrow     Howard Culver
     Packy McCloud                  Fred Howard
     Mesquite Molly                 Gwen Delano
     Trench                         Lou Merrill
     Curley                         Jack Petruzzi
     Josh Lamson                    Parley Baer
     Man (double)                   Malcolm McCoy
     Man 2 (double)                 Malcolm McCoy

108. September 5, 1949              Cry Of The Raven
     Cast:
     Steve Adams/Straight Arrow     Howard Culver
     Packy McCloud                  Fred Howard
     Thundercloud                   Ralph Moody
     Lt Halsey                      Ken Peters
     Colonel                        Ted von Eltz
     Shogun                         Jan Arvin
     Indian (double)                Malcolm McCoy
     ~~Man (double)~~
     ~~Man (double)~~
     Indian 2 (double)              Ken Peters

109.    September 12, 1949            Guns For A Gamble
        Cast:
        Steve Adams/Straight Arrow    Howard Culver
        Packy McCloud                 Fred Howard
        Gonzales
        Shotwell
        Torrent
        Pike
        Doctor (double)
        Jansen (double)

## SPECIAL BROADCAST - SUNDAY

NN      September 18, 1949, Sunday    Buffalo Hunt [7]
        Cast:
        Steve Adams/Straight Arrow    Howard Culver
        Packy McCloud                 Fred Howard
        Sherill Brainard              David Ellis
        Ned Brainard                  Leonard (?) Smith
        Jackdaw Simmons               Charlie Seel

Mondays, Tuesdays & Thursday

110.    September 19, 1949, Monday    Trail Of The Tomahawk
        Cast:
        Steve Adams/Straight Arrow    Howard Culver
        Packy McCloud                 Fred Howard
        Randolph                      Parley Baer
        Voice (double)                Barney Phillips
        Barstow                       Earle Ross
        Hila                          Jan Arvin
        Chief                         Ralph Moody
        Cantrell                      Jack Petruzzi

111.    September 20, 1949, Tuesday   Hunter And Hunted
        Cast:
        Steve Adams/Straight Arrow    Howard Culver
        Packy McCloud                 Fred Howard
        Dallas                        Pinky Parker
        Murdock                       Lou Merrill
        Nekoosa                       Ted von Eltz
        Blue Heron                    Wilms Herbert
        Indian (double)               Malcolm McCoy

112.  September 22, 1949, Thursday  The Beast With The Green Eyes
      Cast:
      Steve Adams/Straight Arrow     Howard Culver
      Packy McCloud                  Fred Howard
      Tuscola                        Lou Krugman
      Bearclaw                       Vic Perrin
      Cutter                         Ken Christy
      Brodie                         David Ellis
      Indian (double)                Nestor Pavia
      Voice (double)                 Nestor Pavia

113.  September 26, 1949, Monday    Without Warning
      Cast:
      Steve Adams/Straight Arrow     Howard Culver
      Packy McCloud                  Fred Howard
      Mesquite Molly                 Gwen Delano
      Carol                          Kay Stewart
      Richie                         Jack Edwards
      Grubstake                      Tim Graham
      Chief                          Bill Green
      Indian (double)                Jan Arvin
      Voice (double)                 Jan Arvin

114.  September 27, 1949, Tuesday   Forest Empire
      Cast:
      Steve Adams/Straight Arrow     Howard Culver
      Packy McCloud                  Fred Howard
      Bull Carnell                   Bill Bouchey
      Squid                          Tyler McVey
      Carabou                        Ralph Moody
      Voice                          J(onathon) Hole, Jr. (?)

115.  September 29, 1949, Thursday  The Triple Cross
      Cast:
      Steve Adams/Straight Arrow     Howard Culver
      Packy McCloud                  Fred Howard
      Burley                         Ken Christy
      Parker                         Earl Lee Huntington
      Cutshaw                        Whitfield Conner
      Vance                          Jack Petruzzi
      Dirk                           Jim Nusser
      Voice (double)                 Jim Nusser

116.  October 3, 1949, Monday       Cattle Crossing
      Cast:
      Steve Adams/Straight Arrow     Howard Culver
      Packy McCloud                  Fred Howard

|  |  |  |
|---|---|---|
|  | Rocklin | Lou Merrill |
|  | Bradley | Parley Baer |
|  | Voice (double) | Tim Graham |
|  | Voice 2 (double) | Stan Waxman |
|  | Dobie | Frank Gerstle |
|  | Stranger (double) | Stan Waxman |
| 117. | October 4, 1949, Tuesday | Long Haul |
|  | Cast: |  |
|  | Steve Adams/Straight Arrow | Howard Culver |
|  | Packy McCloud | Fred Howard |
|  | Jeff | Richard Crenna |
|  | Sheriff | Nestor Paiva |
|  | Skinner | Earle Ross |
|  | Lash | Jack Petruzzi |
|  | Voice (double) | Charlie Lung |
|  | Barstow (double) | Charlie Lung |
|  | Clerk | Nestor Paiva |
| 118. | October 6, 1949, Thursday | The Iron Fist |
|  | Cast: |  |
|  | Steve Adams/Straight Arrow | Howard Culver |
|  | Packy McCloud | Fred Howard |
|  | Iron Fist Devlin | Jack Kruschen |
|  | Roadrunner | Ralph Moody |
|  | Squantem | Jan Arvin |
|  | Sturgess | Parley Baer |
|  | Voice (double) | Jan Arvin |
|  | Voice 2 (double) | Ted von Eltz |
|  | Indian (double) | Ted von Eltz |
| 119. | October 10, 1949, Monday | Dispatch Rider |
|  | Cast: |  |
|  | Steve Adams/Straight Arrow | Howard Culver |
|  | Packy McCloud | Fred Howard |
|  | Mesquite Molly | Gwen Delano |
|  | Sniper | Jack Petruzzi |
|  | Clinch | William Green |
|  | Governor | Parley Baer |
|  | Colonel Carson | Ted von Eltz |
|  | Adanac | Wilms Herbert |
|  | Rider (double) | Wilms Herbert |
|  | Voice 1 (double) | Parley Baer |

120. October 11, 1949, Tuesday Packtrain
 Cast:
 Steve Adams/Straight Arrow Howard Culver
 Packy McCloud Fred Howard
 Sheriff Bailey Ralph Moody
 Dawson Marvin (?) Miller
 Spade Tyler McVey
 Alkali Tim Graham
 Engineer (double) Steve Dunne
 Voice (double) Steve Dunne

121. October 13, 1949, Thursday Lost Water
 Cast:
 Steve Adams/Straight Arrow Howard Culver
 Packy McCloud Fred Howard
 Armand Lou Merrill
 Wilson Ken Christy
 Zachary Charlie Seel
 Slavin Nestor Paiva
 Voice (double) Whitfield Conner

122. October 17, 1949, Monday Smoke-Out
 Cast:
 Steve Adams/Straight Arrow Howard Culver
 Packy McCloud Fred Howard
 Mesquite Molly Gwen Delano
 Vance Lou Krugman
 Scar Jack Petruzzi
 Starfinder Wilms Herbert
 Chief Deercloud Ralph Moody
 Voice (double) Ralph Moody

123. October 18, 1949, Tuesday Greedy Guns
 Cast:
 Steve Adams/Straight Arrow Howard Culver
 Packy McCloud Fred Howard
 Ken Sawyer Whitfield Conner
 Deborah Virginia Gregg
 Cliff Banion Lou Merrill
 Wade Frank Gerstle
 Monte Tim Graham
 Sheriff Joe DuVal

124.  October 20, 1949, Thursday        Shanghaied
      Cast:
      Steve Adams/Straight Arrow        Howard Culver
      Packy McCloud                     Fred Howard
      Dan Walker                        Barton Yarborough
      Bobby Walker                      Johnny McGovern
      Slade                             John Dehner
      Denver                            Vic Perrin
      Man                               Nestor Paiva
      Voice 1 (double)                  Nestor Paiva
      Voice 2 (double)                  Barton Yarborough
      Voice 3 (double)                  Vic Perrin

125.  October 24, 1949, Monday          Hangdog
      Cast:
      Steve Adams/Straight Arrow        Howard Culver
      Packy McCloud                     Fred Howard
      Mesquite Molly                    Gwen Delano
      Chenango                          Richard Crenna
      Decker                            Ken Christy
      Snake                             Jack Petruzzi
      Sheriff                           Charlie Seel
      Yarbio                            Parley Baer
      Man (double)                      Ted von Eltz
      Voice (double)                    Ted von Eltz
      Voice 2 (double)                  Peter Leeds

126.  October 25, 1949, Tuesday         Friend Or Foe
      Cast:
      Steve Adams/Straight Arrow        Howard Culver
      Packy McCloud                     Fred Howard
      Secretary (double)                Malcolm McCoy
      President (double)                Vic Rodman
      Man (double)                      Malcolm McCoy
      Perez                             Nestor Paiva
      Craig                             Lou Merrill
      Dirk                              Tyler McVey
      Officer                           Whitfield Connor

127.  October 27, 1949, Thursday    Gold Of Opar
      Cast:
      Steve Adams/Straight Arrow    Howard Culver
      Packy McCloud                 Fred Howard
      Marshall                      Ralph Moody
      Manger                        John Dehner
      Morlake                       Marvin (?) Miller
      Dirk                          Don Diamond

128.  October 31, 1949, Monday      White Man's Gold
      Cast:
      Steve Adams/Straight Arrow    Howard Culver
      Packy McCloud                 Fred Howard
      Trench                        William (Bill) Bouchey
      Hawkeye                       Wilms Herbert
      Shanty                        Jan Arvin
      Grey Wolf                     Jan Arvin
      Man (double)                  Ralph Moody

129.  November 1, 1949, Tuesday     Passengers For Pecos
      Cast:
      Steve Adams/Straight Arrow    Howard Culver
      Packy McCloud                 Fred Howard
      Mesquite Molly                Gwen Delano
      Craig                         Whitfield Conner
      Bragg                         William Green
      Weasel                        Charles Calvert
      Colonel                       Ted von Eltz
      Crook                         Vic Perrin
      Voice (double)                Charlie Lung
      Officer (double)              Charlie Lung
      Man (double)                  Ted von Eltz
      Indian (double)               Vic Perrin

130.  November 3, 1949, Thursday    Outlaw Siege
      Cast:
      Steve Adams/Straight Arrow    Howard Culver
      Packy McCloud                 Fred Howard
      Leach                         Ben Wright
      Kenesaw                       Lou Merrill
      Carter                        Parley Baer
      Miguel (~~Perez~~)            Harry Bartell
      Slavin                        Charlie Seel
      Navaho (double)               John Stephenson
      Herder (double)               Charlie Seel
      Man (double)                  John Stephenson

131. November 7, 1949, Monday        Stockade
     Cast:
     Steve Adams/Straight Arrow      Howard Culver
     Packy McCloud                   Fred Howard
     Leach                           Ben Wright
     Staley                          Jack Petruzzi
     Spotted Bear                    Vic Perrin
     Kilgore                         John Dehner
     Soldier                         Tim Graham
     Captain                         Parley Baer

132. November 8, 1949, Tuesday       The Brothers
     Cast:
     Steve Adams/Straight Arrow      Howard Culver
     Packy McCloud                   Fred Howard
     Mesquite Molly                  Gwen Delano
     Chet Rawson                     Sam Edwards
     Bat Rawson                      Frank Gerstle
     Voice                           Ralph Moody
     Driver                          Ralph Moody
     Leach                           Ben Wright
     Outlaw                          Jack Kruschen

133. November 10, 1949, Thursday     Sinkhole
     Cast:
     Steve Adams/Straight Arrow      Howard Culver
     Packy McCloud                   Fred Howard
     Leach                           Ben Wright
     Outlaw                          Bill Bouchey
     Lizard                          Wilms Herbert
     Kito                            Jan Arvin
     Voice                           Lou Merrill

134. November 14, 1949, Monday       Foray
     Cast:
     Steve Adams/Straight Arrow      Howard Culver
     Packy McCloud                   Fred Howard
     Foster                          Parley Baer
     Louisa                          Lillian Buyeff
     Bearclaw                        Ralph Moody
     Attwood                         Jack Petruzzi
     Leach                           Ben Wright
     Lookout                         Parley Baer
     Soldier                         Ralph Moody
     Captain                         Ted von Eltz
     Voice                           Ted von Eltz

| 135. | November 15, 1949, Tuesday | The Rescue |
|---|---|---|
| | Cast: | |
| | Steve Adams/Straight Arrow | Howard Culver |
| | Packy McCloud | Fred Howard |
| | Leach | Ben Wright |
| | Spike | Don Diamond |
| | Jim | Jeffrey Silver |
| | Bagby | John Stephenson |
| | Voice | Fred Howard |
| | Voice 2 | Earl Keen |
| | Man | Brad Brown |
| | Dog | Earl Keen |

| 136. | November 17, 1949, Thursday | The Tunnel |
|---|---|---|
| | Cast: | |
| | Steve Adams/Straight Arrow | Howard Culver |
| | Packy McCloud | Fred Howard |
| | Leach | Ben Wright |
| | Esteban | Nestor Paiva |
| | Bart | Ken Christy |
| | Garcia | Nestor Paiva |
| | Voice (double) | Lou Merrill |
| | Voice 2 | Nestor Pavia |

| 137. | November 21, 1949, Monday | Rendezvous |
|---|---|---|
| | Cast: | |
| | Steve Adams/Straight Arrow | Howard Culver |
| | Packy McCloud | Fred Howard |
| | Tracy | Lou Merrill |
| | Trigger | Walter Burke |
| | Grey Fox | Jan Arvin |
| | Sedgecombe | Tudor Owen |
| | Voice | Steve Dunne |

| 138. | November 22, 1949, Tuesday | Showdown |
|---|---|---|
| | Cast: | |
| | Steve Adams/Straight Arrow | Howard Culver |
| | Packy McCloud | Fred Howard |
| | Mesquite Molly | Gwen Delano |
| | Leach | Ben Wright |
| | Sheriff | Ralph Moody |
| | Elkhorn | John Stephenson |

139.  November 24, 1949, Thursday   The Deacon Of Deadwood
      Cast:
      Steve Adams/Straight Arrow   Howard Culver
      Packy McCloud                Fred Howard
      Mesquite Molly               Gwen Delano
      Monty                        Jack Petruzzi
      Voice (double)               Fred Howard
      Deacon                       D. (?) Randolph
      Joe                          Eddie Firestone
      Sheriff                      Parley Baer
      Voice 2                      Parley Baer

140.  November 28, 1949, Monday    Deed Of Grant
      Cast:
      Steve Adams/Straight Arrow   Howard Culver
      Packy McCloud                Fred Howard
      Mesquite Molly               Gwen Delano
      Senora                       Lillian Buyeff
      Miguel                       Byron (?) Kane
      Keeler                       Ken Christy
      Pecos                        Bill Bouchey
      Voice (double)               Nestor Paiva
      Dutch (double)               Jack Petruzzi
      Padre (double)               Nestor Paiva

141.  November 29, 1949, Tuesday   Mustangs And Murder
      Cast:
      Steve Adams/Straight Arrow   Howard Culver
      Packy McCloud                Fred Howard
      Slash                        Lou Merrill
      Bart                         Frank Gerstle
      Guard                        Ralph Moody
      Ahneewok                     Vic Perrin
      Voice                        Malcolm McCoy

142.  December 1, 1949, Thursday   Trail Town
      Cast:
      Steve Adams/Straight Arrow   Howard Culver
      Packy McCloud                Fred Howard
      Vance                        Parley Baer
      Denver                       Ted von Eltz
      Morning                      Jan Arvin
      Doctor                       Whitfield Conner
      Sheriff                      Brad Brown
      Roach                        Walter Burke

143.  December 5, 1949, Monday          Bright Wing (Daughter Of Chief)
      Cast:
      Steve Adams/Straight Arrow        Howard Culver
      Packy McCloud                     Fred Howard
      Mesquite Molly                    Gwen Delano
      Spotted                           John Stephenson
      Tingaya                           Jan Arvin
      Thundercloud                      Ralph Moody
      Bright                            M(?). Shaw
      Indian (double)                   Wilms Herbert

144.  December 6, 1949, Tuesday         Battle Of The Waterhole
      Cast:
      Steve Adams/Straight Arrow        Howard Culver
      Packy McCloud                     Fred Howard
      Lance                             Walter Burke
      Trig                              John Dehner
      Rogers                            Tim Graham
      Pearson                           Ted von Eltz
      Sheriff                           Earl Lee
      Voice (double)                    John Dehner

145.  December 8, 1949, Thursday        Big Talk (Tall Talk)
      Cast:
      Steve Adams/Straight Arrow        Howard Culver
      Packy McCloud                     Fred Howard
      Jeff                              Sam Edwards
      Washoe                            Jack Petruzzi
      Daley                             Lou Merrill
      Dade                              Cliff Arquette
      Sheriff                           Parley Baer

146.  December 12, 1949, Monday         Hidden Danger
      Cast:
      Steve Adams/Straight Arrow        Howard Culver
      Packy McCloud                     Fred Howard
      Mesquite Molly                    Gwen Delano
      Sanford                           Parley Baer
      Trask                             Jack Petruzzi
      Craley                            Walter Burke

Straight Arrow Radio Log 67

147.  December 13, 1949, Tuesday    Burn-Out
      Cast:
      Steve Adams/Straight Arrow     Howard Culver
      Packy McCloud                  Fred Howard
      Spike                          Don Diamond
      Lars                           Robert Bruce
      Inge                           Jane Webb
      Eric                           Jeffrey Silver
      Logan                          Lou Merrill
      ~~Snake~~
      Sheriff                        Cy Kendell
      Voice (double - twice)         Robert Bruce

148.  December 15, 1949, Thursday   The Big Cat
      Cast:
      Steve Adams/Straight Arrow     Howard Culver
      Packy McCloud                  Fred Howard
      Dakon                          William Bouchey
      Parker                         Ralph Moody
      Cheekaw                        Ted von Eltz
      Denver                         Whitfield Connor
      Voice                          Jan Arvin

149.  December 19, 1949, Monday     Call For Help
      Cast:
      Steve Adams/Straight Arrow     Howard Culver
      Packy McCloud                  Fred Howard
      Mesquite Molly                 Gwen Delano
      Dexter                         Earle Ross
      Pasco                          Jack Petruzzi
      Driver                         Charlie Lung
      Indian                         Vic Perrin
      Langhorn                       Parley Baer
      Groom                          Charlie Lung

150.  December 20, 1949, Tuesday    Tenderfoot
      Cast:
      Steve Adams/Straight Arrow     Howard Culver
      Packy McCloud                  Fred Howard
      Santee                         William (Bill) Bouchey
      Belcher                        Charles Calvert
      Wilkins                        Ted von Eltz
      Sheriff                        Ralph Moody

151.  December 22, 1949, Thursday   The Strong Bow
      Cast:
      Steve Adams/Straight Arrow     Howard Culver
      Packy McCloud                  Fred Howard
      Jeff                           Ken Christy
      Lynch                          Frank Gerstle
      Snavely                        Walter Burke
      Jacobs                         Lou Merrill
      Voice                          Nestor Paiva
      Voice 2                        Lou Merrill
      Voice 3                        Harry Bartell
      Voice 4                        Nestor Paiva

152.  December 26, 1949, Monday      Deception Council
      Cast:
      Steve Adams/Straight Arrow     Howard Culver
      Packy McCloud                  Fred Howard
      Bart                           (no name listed)
      Flint                          William Green
      Blake                          Parley Baer
      ~~Skyland~~
      Soldier                        Richard Crenna
      Paymaster                      Tim Graham
      Voice                          Tim Graham

153.  December 27, 1949, Tuesday     Land Of Mist
      Cast:
      Steve Adams/Straight Arrow     Howard Culver
      Packy McCloud                  Fred Howard
      Mesquite Molly                 Gwen Delano
      Latigo                         William (Bill) Bouchey
      Bowie                          Jack Petruzzi
      Scanlon                        Walter Burke
      Marshall                       B(?). Browne
      Voice                          Malcolm McCoy

154.  December 29, 1949, Thursday    Hide-Away
      Cast:
      Steve Adams/Straight Arrow     Howard Culver
      Packy McCloud                  Fred Howard
      Welch                          Lou Merrill
      Carson                         Tyler McVey
      Langley                        Ted von Eltz
      Meeker                         Whitfield Connor
      Antelope                       Ralph Moody
      Sheriff                        Cliff Arquette
      Man (double)                   Ralph Moody

## MUTUAL BROADCASTING SYSTEM - 1950

155. January 2, 1950, Monday         The Leader
     Cast:
     Steve Adams/Straight Arrow       Howard Culver
     Packy McCloud                    Fred Howard
     Rufus                            Ken Christy
     Woman                            Connie Crowder
     Trench                           John Stephenson
     Skywak                           Tom Holland
     Nails                            Jack Petruzzi
     Chief                            Ralph Moody
     Man                              Ralph Moody

156. January 3, 1950, Tuesday        The Dressmaker From Dusty Bend
     Cast:
     Steve Adams/Straight Arrow       Howard Culver
     Packy McCloud                    Fred Howard
     Mesquite Molly                   Gwen Delano
     Hazel                            Virginia Gregg
     Gordon                           Walter Burke
     Giles                            Frank Parker
     Marshall                         Tim Graham

157. January 5, 1950, Thursday       The Blacksnake Whip
     Cast:
     Steve Adams/Straight Arrow       Howard Culver
     Packy McCloud                    Fred Howard
     Harvey                           Eric Lord
     Bender                           Lou Merrill
     Sheriff                          Parley Baer
     Mack                             Nestor Paiva

158. January 9, 1950, Monday         Turn Of The Tide
     Cast:
     Steve Adams/Straight Arrow       Howard Culver
     Packy McCloud                    Fred Howard
     Slash                            William (Bill) Bouchey
     Bullock                          Jack Petruzzi
     Carlos                           Nestor Paiva
     Wilkins                          Parley Baer
     Voice (double)                   Jan Arvin
     Voice (double-2)                 Jan Arvin

159.  January 10, 1950, Tuesday         The Trap
      Cast:
      Steve Adams/Straight Arrow        Howard Culver
      Packy McCloud                     Fred Howard
      Mesquite Molly                    Gwen Delano
      Saddler                           Richard Crenna
      Marshall                          Ralph Moody
      Denver                            Walter Burke
      Craven                            Ken Christy
      Voice (double)                    S(?). Roberts
      Voice (double - 2)                Ralph Moody

160.  January 12, 1950, Thursday        Trail's End (The Superstitions)
      Cast:
      Steve Adams/Straight Arrow        Howard Culver
      Packy McCloud                     Fred Howard
      Pritchard                         Ted von Eltz
      Scully                            John Dehner
      Tatum                             William Green
      Gilespie                          L. J. Heydt (?)
      Voice                             Lou Merrill
      Harper                            John Dehner

161.  January 16, 1950, Monday          The Ring
      Cast:
      Steve Adams/Straight Arrow        Howard Culver
      Packy McCloud                     Fred Howard
      Sorley                            Lou Merrill
      Jaguar                            Vic Perrin
      Abinango                          Ralph Moody
      Bartender                         Steve Dunne
      Chisolm                           Jack Petruzzi
      Voice                             Steve Dunne

162.  January 17, 1950, Tuesday         The Captive
      Cast:
      Steve Adams/Straight Arrow        Howard Culver
      Packy McCloud                     Fred Howard
      Mesquite Molly                    Gwen Delano
      Pollack                           William (Bill) Bouchey
      Kracken                           Walter Burke
      Mandota                           William Green
      Indian                            Jan Arvin

163. January 19, 1950, Thursday          Great Bear
     Cast:
     Steve Adams/Straight Arrow          Howard Culver
     Packy McCloud                       Fred Howard
     Eagle                               D. Oreck (?)
     Mane                                Ted von Eltz
     Snare                               Ken Christy
     Bigahway                            Wilms Herbert
     Bear                                Earl Keen

164. January 23, 1950, Monday            Double Hostage
     Cast:
     Steve Adams/Straight Arrow          Howard Culver
     Packy McCloud                       Fred Howard
     Indian                              Jack Petruzzi
     Jaguar                              Vic Perrin
     Sheriff                             Parley Baer
     Sorley                              Lou Merrill
     Lizard                              Jan Arvin
     Abinango                            Ralph Moody
     Indian (2 double)                   Jack Petruzzi

165. January 24, 1950, Tuesday           Rampage
     Cast:
     Steve Adams/Straight Arrow          Howard Culver
     Packy McCloud                       Fred Howard
     Mesquite Molly                      Gwen Delano
     Jaguar                              Vic Perrin
     Woman                               Connie Crowder
     Man                                 Jan Arvin
     Logan                               Vic Perrin
     Woman 2                             Virginia Gregg
     Man 2                               Malcolm McCoy
     Sarah                               Virginia Gregg
     Bailey                              Whit Connor
     Grey Lizard                         Jan Arvin
     Sheriff                             Bruce (?) Payne

166.  January 26, 1950, Thursday      The Map
      Cast:
      Steve Adams/Straight Arrow      Howard Culver
      Packy McCloud                   Fred Howard
      Jaguar                          Vic Perrin
      Tumble                          Cliff Arquette
      Murdock                         Herb Butterfield
      Slagle                          Walter Burke
      Sheriff                         Tim Graham

167.  January 30, 1950, Monday        Flaming Guns
      Cast:
      Steve Adams/Straight Arrow      Howard Culver
      Packy McCloud                   Fred Howard
      Wade                            John Dehner
      Taggett                         Parley Baer
      Rankin                          William Bouchey
      Savage                          Jack Petruzzi
      Chisholm                        Earl Lee Huntington
      Voice (double)                  Lou Merrill

168.  January 31, 1950, Tuesday       Ghost Mountain
      Cast:
      Steve Adams/Straight Arrow      Howard Culver
      Packy McCloud                   Fred Howard
      Hook                            Joe Duval
      Trigger                         Walter Burke
      Voice (double)                  Jack Baston
      Indian                          Tom Holland
      Sheriff                         Tim Graham
      Abinango                        Ralph Moody
      Kittredge                       Ted von Eltz
      Man                             Jack Baston
      Man 2                           Tom Holland
      Man 3                           Ted von Eltz

169.  February 2, 1950, Thursday      Masquerade For Murder
      Cast:
      Steve Adams/Straight Arrow      Howard Culver
      Packy McCloud                   Fred Howard
      Mesquite Molly                  Gwen Delano
      Driver                          Barney Phillips
      Lacey                           Ken Christy
      Sheriff                         Junius Matthews
      Voice (double)                  Barney Phillips
      Creevy                          Frank Gerstle
      Voice 2                         Nestor Paiva

Tuesday 5 - 5:30 PM
Thursday 5 - 5:30 PM

170.   February 7, 1950, Tuesday        Sands Of Gold
       Cast:
       Steve Adams/Straight Arrow       Howard Culver
       Packy McCloud                    Fred Howard
       Nugent                           Fred (?) Shields
       Torrent                          Tim McVey
       Sheriff                          Tim Graham
       Tumbleweed                       Cliff Arquette
       Abinango                         Ralph Moody
       Voice (~~double~~)               Lou Merrill

171.   February 9, 1950, Thursday       Dead Man Swindle
       Cast:
       Steve Adams/Straight Arrow       Howard Culver
       Packy McCloud                    Fred Howard
       Mesquite Molly                   Gwen Delano
       Deborah                          Lillian Buyeff
       Slaughter                        Earle Ross
       Frank                            Whit Connor
       Sheriff                          Brad Brown
       Voice (double)                   Walter Burke
       Dragoe                           Jack Petruzzi
       Voice 2 (double)                 Walter Burke

172.   8

173.   February 14, 1950, Tuesday       The Creek
       Cast:
       Steve Adams/Straight Arrow       Howard Culver
       Packy McCloud                    Fred Howard
       Voice                            Earl Lee Huntington
       Shanty                           Lou Merrill
       Chalmers                         Richard Crenna
       Jason                            Jack Petruzzi
       Assayer                          Malcolm McCoy
       Sheriff                          Ted von Eltz

174. February 16, 1950, Thursday    Left Hand, Right Hand
Cast:
Steve Adams/Straight Arrow    Howard Culver
Packy McCloud    Fred Howard
Mesquite Molly    Gwen Delano
Bart
Sheriff
Lanier
Tehano
Indian

175. February 21, 1950, Tuesday    The Badge
Cast:
Steve Adams/Straight Arrow    Howard Culver
Packy McCloud    Fred Howard
Wilkins    Robert Bruce
Slavin    William (Bill) Bouchey
Dirk    Nestor Paiva
Snake    Jack Petruzzi

176. February 23, 1950, Thursday    Money To Burn
Cast:
Steve Adams/Straight Arrow    Howard Culver
Packy McCloud    Fred Howard
Mesquite Molly    Gwen Delano
Wichataw    Cliff Arquette
Sheriff    Parley Baer
Skull    Ken Christy
Wilkie    Ralph Moody

177. February 28, 1950, Tuesday    Treaty Trouble
Cast:
Steve Adams/Straight Arrow    Howard Culver
Packy McCloud    Fred Howard
Lawson    Ted von Eltz
Hardtack    Lou Merrill
Running Buffalo    Ralph Moody
Officer    Jack Petruzzi

178. March 2, 1950, Thursday    Skin Deep
Cast:
Steve Adams/Straight Arrow    Howard Culver
Packy McCloud    Fred Howard
Mesquite Molly    Gwen Delano
Penny    Anne Diamond
Chandler    Olan Soulé

|  |  |  |
|---|---|---|
|  | Warlock | John Dehner |
|  | Utah | Walter Burke |
|  | Saddler | Parley Baer |
|  | Sheriff | John Frank |
|  | Voice | Parley Baer |
| 179. | March 7, 1950, Tuesday | Gunpower Trail |
|  | Cast: |  |
|  | Steve Adams/Straight Arrow | Howard Culver |
|  | Packy McCloud | Fred Howard |
|  | Sanders | Tudor Owen |
|  | Link | Walter Burke |
|  | Spider | William Bouchey |
|  | Sheriff | Tim Graham |
|  | Dakota | Ralph Moody |
|  | Voice (double) | Ralph Moody |
| 180. | March 9, 1950, Thursday | Scourge |
|  | Cast: |  |
|  | Steve Adams/Straight Arrow | Howard Culver |
|  | Packy McCloud | Fred Howard |
|  | Mesquite Molly | Gwen Delano |
|  | Hawthorne | Parley Baer |
|  | Rackley | Nestor Paiva |
|  | Spike | Jack Petruzzi |
|  | Voice | Jan Arvin |
|  | Women | Florence Ravenal |
|  | Voice #2 | Parley Baer |
|  | Women #2 | Florence Ravenal |
| 181. | March 14, 1950, Tuesday | Stolen Stallion |
|  | Cast: |  |
|  | Steve Adams/Straight Arrow | Howard Culver |
|  | Packy McCloud | Fred Howard |
|  | Clayton | Whit Connor |
|  | Nancy | Lillian Buyeff |
|  | Racey | Lou Merrill |
|  | Dirk | Tyler McVey |
|  | Voice (double) | Jack Petruzzi |

182. March 16, 1950, Thursday    The Carpetbag
Cast:
Steve Adams/Straight Arrow    Howard Culver
Packy McCloud    Fred Howard
Mesquite Molly    Gwen Delano
Tanner    Bill Bouchey
Mohave    Charlie Seel
Leegahno    Ralph Moody
Driver    Vic Perrin
Indian    Vic Perrin
Voice    Ralph Moody

183. March 21, 1950, Tuesday    Blow Up
Cast:
Steve Adams/Straight Arrow    Howard Culver
Packy McCloud    Fred Howard
Donneger    Harry Bartell
Catlett    Bill Bouchey
Windy    Wilms Herbert
Manager    Ralph Moody
Voice 1    Ralph Moody
Voice 2    Nestor Paiva
Voice 3    Malcolm McCoy
Voice 4    Harry Bartell

184. March 23, 1950, Thursday    Bitter Creek Station
Cast:
Steve Adams/Straight Arrow    Howard Culver
Packy McCloud    Fred Howard
Mesquite Molly    Gwen Delano
Barry    Whit Connor
Groat    Walter Burke
Koster    Jack Petruzzi
Spanner    Bill Green
Amanda    Connie Crowder
Woman    Connie Crowder
Man    Brad Brown
Sheriff    Brad Brown
Driver    Bill Green

185. March 28, 1950, Tuesday    Fighter Without Guns
Cast:
Steve Adams/Straight Arrow    Howard Culver
Packy McCloud    Fred Howard
Mesquite Molly    Gwen Delano
Parson    Donald Woods

|      |                         |                 |
|------|-------------------------|-----------------|
|      | Spade                   | Lou Merrill     |
|      | Quirt                   | Pinky Parker    |
|      | Fargo                   | Herb Ellis      |
|      | Man                     | Ralph Moody     |
|      | Man 2                   | Herb Ellis      |
|      | Man 3                   | Ralph Moody     |
|      | Woman                   | Kay Stewart     |
| 186. | March 30, 1950, Thursday | Bellwether     |
|      | Cast:                   |                 |
|      | Steve Adams/Straight Arrow | Howard Culver |
|      | Packy McCloud           | Fred Howard     |
|      | Ramon                   | Nestor Paiva    |
|      | Gibson                  | Charlie Seel    |
|      | Squires                 | Parley Baer     |
|      | Voice                   | Jack Petruzzi   |
|      | Voice 2                 | Jan Arvin       |
|      | Voice 3                 | Ted von Eltz    |
| 187. | April 4, 1950, Tuesday  | The Crooked Trail |
|      | Cast:                   |                 |
|      | Steve Adams/Straight Arrow | Howard Culver |
|      | Packy McCloud           | Fred Howard     |
|      | Scurlock                | Lou Merrill     |
|      | Jed                     | Herb Butterfield |
|      | Buck                    | Walter Burke    |
|      | Chief                   | Ralph Moody     |
|      | Dealer                  | Hal Dawson      |
|      | Voice (double)          | Ralph Moody     |
| 188. | April 6, 1950, Thursday | Thieves Fall Out |
|      | Cast:                   |                 |
|      | Steve Adams/Straight Arrow | Howard Culver |
|      | Packy McCloud           | Fred Howard     |
|      | Mesquite Molly          | Gwen Delano     |
|      | Colter                  | John Dehner     |
|      | Dade                    | Bill Bouchey    |
|      | Gimlet                  | Jack Petruzzi   |
|      | Sheriff                 | Parley Baer     |

189. April 11, 1950, Tuesday          Buffalo Trace
     Cast:
     Steve Adams/Straight Arrow       Howard Culver
     Packy McCloud                    Fred Howard
     Musker                           Ken Christy
     Crooks                           Herb Ellis
     Kigaya                           Ralph Moody
     Wagner                           Whit Connor
     Sheriff                          Brad Brown
     Voice                            Ralph Moody
     Indian                           Jan Arvin
     Voice 2                          Jan Arvin

190. April 13, 1950, Thursday         Run For Your Money
     Cast:
     Steve Adams/Straight Arrow       Howard Culver
     Packy McCloud                    Fred Howard
     Mesquite Molly                   Gwen Delano
     Carl (Holstrom)                  Tim Graham
     Tack (Sloan)                     Tyler McVey
     Digger                           Frank Gerstle
     Woman                            Connie Crowder
     Voice                            Tim Graham
     Voice 2                          Parley Baer

191. April 18, 1950, Tuesday          Loaded For Bear
     Cast:
     Steve Adams/Straight Arrow       Howard Culver
     Packy McCloud                    Fred Howard
     Mesquite Molly                   Gwen Delano
     Monk                             Jack Petruzzi
     Jessup                           Lou Merrill
     Ritchif                          Eddie Firestone
     Sheriff                          Olan Soulé

192. April 20, 1950, Thursday         The Wampun
     Cast:
     Steve Adams/Straight Arrow       Howard Culver
     Packy McCloud                    Fred Howard
     Townsend                         Parley Baer
     Lynch                            Bill Bouchey
     Raglin                           Vic Perrin
     Black                            Walter Burke
     Strawbridge                      Ralph Moody
     Indian                           Ralph Moody

| | | |
|---|---|---|
| 193. | April 25, 1950, Tuesday | False Feathers |
| | Cast: | |
| | Steve Adams/Straight Arrow | Howard Culver |
| | Packy McCloud | Fred Howard |
| | Murdock | Earle Ross |
| | Hagley | Charlie Seel |
| | Lynch | Bill Bouchey |
| | Lawson | Whitfield Connor |
| | Frazer | Tim Graham |
| | Voice | Nestor Paiva |
| | | |
| 194. | April 27, 1950, Thursday | Gunsight Notch |
| | Cast: | |
| | Steve Adams/Straight Arrow | Howard Culver |
| | Packy McCloud | Fred Howard |
| | Mesquite Molly | Gwen Delano |
| | Anton | John Dehner |
| | Bleak | Harry Bartell |
| | Spade | Ken Christy |
| | Voice | Jan Arvin |
| | Indian | Jan Arvin |
| | Voice 2 | Harry Bartell |
| | | |
| 195. | May 2, 1950, Tuesday | Dynamite Ledge |
| | Cast: | |
| | Steve Adams/Straight Arrow | Howard Culver |
| | Packy McCloud | Fred Howard |
| | Mesquite Molly | Gwen Delano |
| | Skull | Lou Merrill |
| | Nails | Herb Ellis |
| | Voice | Jack Petruzzi |
| | Danker | Ted von Eltz |
| | Larson | Bob Bruce |
| | Voice 2 | Jack Petruzzi |
| | | |
| 196. | May 4, 1950, Thursday | Deep River |
| | Cast: | |
| | Steve Adams/Straight Arrow | Howard Culver |
| | Packy McCloud | Fred Howard |
| | Spider | Walter Burke |
| | Lynch | Bill Bouchey |
| | Shogun | Ralph Moody |
| | Grady | Parley Baer |
| | Welch (double by Shogun) | Ralph Moody |
| | Voice (double by Lynch) | Bill Bouchey |

197.  May 9, 1950, Tuesday          Fire And (Flood) Water
      Cast:
      Steve Adams/Straight Arrow    Howard Culver
      Packy McCloud                 Fred Howard
      Purdy                         Junius Matthews
      Flint                         Tyler McVey
      Lynch                         Bill Bouchey
      Johnson                       Herb Butterfield
      Hazen                         Jan Arvin
      Indian                        Herb Butterfield
      Buffalo Hide                  Jan Arvin

198.  May 11, 1950, Thursday        Iron Spike
      Cast:
      Steve Adams/Straight Arrow    Howard Culver
      Packy McCloud                 Fred Howard
      Mesquite Molly                Gwen Delano
      Lynch                         Bill Bouchey
      Jarvis                        Jack Petruzzi
      Townsend                      Parley Baer
      Indian                        Bill Green

199.  May 16, 1950, Tuesday         Fight For The Flag
      Cast:
      Steve Adams/Straight Arrow    Howard Culver
      Packy McCloud                 Fred Howard
      Mesquite Molly                Gwen Delano
      Dan                           Olan Soulé
      Amanda                        Lillian Buyeff
      Lynch                         Bill Bouchey
      Outlaw                        Lou Merrill
      Women                         Lillian Buyeff
      Voice                         Lou Merrill

200.  May 18, 1950, Thursday        Escape
      Cast:
      Steve Adams/Straight Arrow    Howard Culver
      Packy McCloud                 Fred Howard
      Lynch                         Bill Bouchey
      Dagger                        Walter Burke
      Badger                        Frances X. Bushman
      Sheriff                       Parley Baer
      Voice                         Malcolm McCoy
      Conductor                     Parley Baer
      Lieutenant                    Malcolm McCoy

| 201. | May 23, 1950, Tuesday | Dead Creek |
| --- | --- | --- |
|  | Cast: |  |
|  | Steve Adams/Straight Arrow | Howard Culver |
|  | Packy McCloud | Fred Howard |
|  | Bat Mahoney | Tyler McVey |
|  | Dave | Whit Connor |
|  | Sarah | Virginia Gregg |
|  | Slade | Jack Petruzzi |
|  | Voice | Earl Lee |
|  | Voice 2 | Whit Connor |
| 202. | May 25, 1950, Thursday | Secret Stage |
|  | Cast: |  |
|  | Steve Adams/Straight Arrow | Howard Culver |
|  | Packy McCloud | Fred Howard |
|  | Mesquite Molly | Gwen Delano |
|  | Sparrow | Parley Baer |
|  | Ace | Vic Perrin |
|  | Cantrell | Ken Christy |
|  | Sheriff | Ralph Moody |
| 203. | May 30, 1950, Tuesday | Cartwheel |
|  | Cast: |  |
|  | Steve Adams/Straight Arrow | Howard Culver |
|  | Packy McCloud | Fred Howard |
|  | Tasco | Lou Merrill |
|  | Cartwheel | Jack Petruzzi |
|  | Rod | Harry Bartell |
|  | Nancy | Jane Webb |
|  | Nevada | Nestor Paiva |
|  | Voice | Brad Brown |
| 204. | June 1, 1950, Thursday | The Paper |
|  | Cast: |  |
|  | Steve Adams/Straight Arrow | Howard Culver |
|  | Packy McCloud | Fred Howard |
|  | Mesquite Molly | Gwen Delano |
|  | Mousey | Howard McNear |
|  | Lije | Ralph Moody |
|  | Savage | Walter Burke |
|  | Trig | Herb Ellis |
|  | Turquoise | Jeffrey Silver |
|  | Man | Fred Howard |

205. June 6, 1950, Tuesday         Pay Dirt
     Cast:
     Steve Adams/Straight Arrow    Howard Culver
     Packy McCloud                 Fred Howard
     Rickey                        Whit Connor
     Bettina                       Kay Stewart
     Jacklin                       Ralph Sanford
     Slag                          Frank Gerstle

206. June 8, 1950, Thursday        Renegade Rustler
     Cast:
     Steve Adams/Straight Arrow    Howard Culver
     Packy McCloud                 Fred Howard
     Mesquite Molly                Gwen Delano
     Ben                           Olan Soulé
     Sarah                         Lillian Buyeff
     Latigo                        Ken Christy
     Sheriff                       Parley Baer
     Dirk                          Jack Petruzzi
     Voice                         Ralph Moody
     Indian                        Ralph Moody

207. June 13, 1950, Tuesday        Face Of Danger
     Cast:
     Steve Adams/Straight Arrow    Howard Culver
     Packy McCloud                 Fred Howard
     Mesquite Molly                Gwen Delano
     Peter Goad                    Jeffrey Silver
     Jason                         Ted von Eltz
     Bart                          Lou Merrill
     Pike                          Jack Petruzzi
     Driver                        Malcolm McCoy
     Sheriff                       Malcolm McCoy

208. June 15, 1950, Thursday       Line Of Duty
     Cast:
     Steve Adams/Straight Arrow    Howard Culver
     Packy McCloud                 Fred Howard
     Sanders                       Dick Crenna
     Scorpin                       Bill Green
     Concho                        Joe DuVal
     Sergeant                      Tim Graham
     Colonel                       Parley Baer
     Man                           Parley Baer

209.  June 20, 1950, Tuesday          Desert Riches
      Cast:
      Steve Adams/Straight Arrow      Howard Culver
      Packy McCloud                   Fred Howard
      Mesquite Molly                  Gwen Delano
      Miquel                          Nestor Paiva
      Deuce                           Walter Burke
      Stag                            Herb Ellis
      Sheriff                         Ralph Moody
      Man                             Nestor Paiva
      Man 2                           Ralph Moody

210.  June 22, 1950, Thursday         Moccasin Print
      Cast:
      Steve Adams/Straight Arrow      Howard Culver
      Packy McCloud                   Fred Howard
      Jed                             Parley Baer
      Abby                            Connie Crowder
      Butcher                         Jack Petruzzi
      Rattler                         Ken Christy
      Ogitahway                       Pedro de Cordova
      Voice                           Pedro de Cordova

## SUMMER BREAK $_9$, 1950

211.  September 12, Tuesday Repeat Show

212.  September 14, Thursday Repeat Show

213.  September 19, Tuesday Repeat Show

214.  September 21, Thursday Repeat Show

215.  September 26, Tuesday           Deserter
      Cast:
      Steve Adams/Straight Arrow      Howard Culver
      Packy McCloud                   Fred Howard
      Running Deer
      Spade
      Pike
      Colonel
      Man, Man 2, Sergeant (doubles)

216.  September 28, 1950, Thursday  Return Of The Snake
      Cast: No additional information available

217.  October 3, 1950, Tuesday         Border Bandits
      Cast:
      Steve Adams/Straight Arrow       Howard Culver
      Packy McCloud                    Fred Howard
      Calhoun
      Killgrew
      Spider
      Slavin
      Colonel, Man, Man 2 (doubles)

218.  October 5, 1950, Thursday        Pay Wagon
      Cast:
      Steve Adams/Straight Arrow       Howard Culver
      Packy McCloud                    Fred Howard
      Mesquite Molly                   Gwen Delano
      Calhoun                          Whit Connor
      Billy                            Eddie Firestone
      Abel                             Ralph Moody
      Spike                            Ken Christy
      Nailer                           Vic Perrin
      Man                              Vic Perrin
      Man 2                            Ralph Moody
      Man 3                            Whit Connor
      Woman                            Vivi Janiss

219.  October 10, 1950, Tuesday        Sign Of The Dagger
      Cast:
      Steve Adams/Straight Arrow       Howard Culver
      Packy McCloud                    Fred Howard
      Mesquite Molly                   Gwen Delano
      Calhoun                          Whit Connor
      Dave                             Olan Soulé
      Betsy                            Virginia Gregg
      Torrent                          Bill Bouchey
      Snake                            Tyler McVey
      Man                              Tyler McVey
      Man 2                            Malcolm McCoy
      Man 3                            Malcolm McCoy
      Woman                            Virginia Gregg

220.  October 12, 1950, Thursday       Precious Pebbles
      Cast:
      Steve Adams/Straight Arrow       Howard Culver
      Packy McCloud                    Fred Howard
      Calhoun                          Whit Connor
      Bob                              Dick Crenna
      Wilkins                          Bill Green
      Savage                           Frank Gerstle

221.  October 17, 1950, Tuesday        Recruit
      Cast:
      Steve Adams/Straight Arrow       Howard Culver
      Packy McCloud                    Fred Howard
      Calhoun                          Whit Connor
      Roger                            Jonathan Hole
      Rocky                            John Dehner
      Weasel                           Franklin Parker
      Latigahna                        Ralph Moody
      Soldier                          Ralph Moody

222.  October 19, 1950, Thursday       Honor Of The Regiment
      Cast:
      Steve Adams/Straight Arrow       Howard Culver
      Packy McCloud                    Fred Howard
      Mesquite Molly                   Gwen Delano
      Calhoun                          Whit Connor
      Mangrun                          Ted von Eltz
      Bullock                          Ken Christy
      Colonel                          Frances X. Bushman
      Soldier                          Tim Graham
      Lieutenant (double)              Ted von Eltz
      Man (double)                     Whit Connor
      Man 2 (double)                   Tim Graham

223.  October 24, 1950, Tuesday        Red Feather
      Cast:
      Steve Adams/Straight Arrow       Howard Culver
      Packy McCloud                    Fred Howard
      Bailey                           Tudor Owen
      Marsters                         Lou Merrill
      Bearpaw                          Jan Arvin
      Slaughter                        Barney Phillips

224.  October 26, 1950, Thursday       Helping Hand
      Cast:
      Steve Adams/Straight Arrow       Howard Culver
      Packy McCloud                    Fred Howard
      Mesquite Molly                   Gwen Delano
      Levi                             Earl Lee
      Sellers                          Tyler McVey
      Pike                             Ed Max
      Man #1                           Cliff Arquette
      Man #2                           Brad Brown

225.  October 31, 1950, Tuesday         Avalanche
      Cast:
      Steve Adams/Straight Arrow        Howard Culver
      Packy McCloud                     Fred Howard
      Kreech                            Ken Christy
      Dallas                            Vic Perrin
      Nancy                             Marion Richman
      Woodbridge                        Ralph Moody
      Parsons                           Ted von Eltz
      Man 1 (double)                    Ralph Moody
      Man 2 (double)                    Ralph Moody
      Woman (double)                    Marion Richman

226.  November 2, 1950, Thursday        Candlewick
      Cast:
      Steve Adams/Straight Arrow        Howard Culver
      Packy McCloud                     Fred Howard
      Mesquite Molly                    Gwen Delano
      Rachel                            Connie Crowder
      Ben                               Malcolm McCoy
      Flint                             John Dehner
      Lynch                             Herb Ellis

227.  November 7, 1950, Tuesday         The People's Choice
      Cast:
      Steve Adams/Straight Arrow        Howard Culver
      Packy McCloud                     Fred Howard
      Bartlett                          Parley Baer
      Clawson                           Lou Merrill
      Welch                             Ty McVey
      Lacey                             Nestor Paiva
      Man                               Tim Graham
      Man 2                             Stan Ferrar

228.  November 9, 1950, Thursday        Trail By Fire
      Cast:
      Steve Adams/Straight Arrow        Howard Culver
      Packy McCloud                     Fred Howard
      Mesquite Molly                    Gwen Delano
      Robby                             Jeffrey Silver
      Blackie                           Lou Krugman
      Slavin                            Bill Bouchey
      Partridge                         Olan Soulé
      Sheriff                           Ralph Moody
      Stage Driver                      Ralph Moody

229.  November 14, 1950, Tuesday    Mark Of The (Arrow) Outlaw
      Cast:
      Steve Adams/Straight Arrow    Howard Culver
      Packy McCloud                 Fred Howard
      Kinder                        Ken Christy
      Rawhide                       Lamont Johnson
      Antelope                      Jan Arvin
      Lawson                        Herb Butterfield
      Man                           Barney Phillips
      Man #2                        Jan Arvin

230.  November 16, 1950, Thursday   Reflected Glory
      Cast:
      Steve Adams/Straight Arrow    Howard Culver
      Packy McCloud                 Fred Howard
      Mesquite Molly                Gwen Delano
      Silas                         Cliff Arquette
      Gurney                        John Dehner
      Catlett                       Herb Ellis
      Man                           Herb Ellis
      Man 2                         Fred Howard
      Man 3                         Cliff Arquette

231.  November 21, 1950, Tuesday    Winding River
      Cast:
      Steve Adams/Straight Arrow    Howard Culver
      Packy McCloud                 Fred Howard
      Frenchy                       Lou Merrill
      Tealwing                      Vic Perrin
      Pritchard                     Bill Bouchey
      Chelsoe                       Wilms Herbert
      Voice                         Vic Perrin

232.  November 23, 1950, Thursday   Golden Harvest
      Cast:
      Steve Adams/Straight Arrow    Howard Culver
      Packy McCloud                 Fred Howard
      Mesquite Molly                Gwen Delano
      Widow                         Virginia Gregg
      Daley                         Parley Baer
      Link                          Tyler McVey
      Scar                          Ralph Moody

233.  November 28, 1950, Tuesday    Big Talk
      Cast:
      Steve Adams/Straight Arrow     Howard Culver
      Packy McCloud                  Fred Howard
      Mesquite Molly                 Gwen Delano
      Daley                          Parley Baer
      Slick                          John Dehner
      Jasper                         Lou Krugman
      Sheriff                        Malcolm McCoy
      Man                            Malcolm McCoy
      Man 2                          Tim Graham

234.  November 30, 1950, Thursday   Warning Ring
      Cast:
      Steve Adams/Straight Arrow     Howard Culver
      Packy McCloud                  Fred Howard
      Sam (Daley)                    Parley Baer
      Michael                        Stuffy Singer
      Montana                        Ken Christy
      Bella                          Rena Craig
      Man                            Bill Green

235.  December 5, 1950, Tuesday     Heirloom Of Gold
      Cast:
      Steve Adams/Straight Arrow     Howard Culver
      Packy McCloud                  Fred Howard
      Mesquite Molly                 Gwen Delano
      Medicine Man                   Ralph Moody
      Sam (Daley)                    Parley Baer
      Bull                           Bill Bouchey
      Doc                            Ralph Moody
      Man                            Nestor Paiva
      Bartender                      Parley Baer
      Spade                          Nestor Paiva

236.  December 7, 1950, Thursday    Eagle Pass
      Cast:
      Steve Adams/Straight Arrow     Howard Culver
      Packy McCloud                  Fred Howard
      Scorpion                       Bob Griffin
      Gruber                         Lou Merrill
      Dirk                           Herb Ellis
      Man                            Frank Gerstle
      Man 2                          Herb Ellis

237. December 12, 1950, Tuesday    False Trail
     Cast:
     Steve Adams/Straight Arrow    Howard Culver
     Packy McCloud                 Fred Howard
     Mesquite Molly                Gwen Delano
     Scorpion                      Robert Griffin
     Calkins                       John Dehner
     Woman                         Constance Crowder
     Man                           Tim Graham
     Man 2                         Tim Graham
     Man 3                         John Dehner
     Sheriff                       Malcolm McCoy

238. December 14, 1950, Thursday   The Unmasked
     Cast:
     Steve Adams/Straight Arrow    Howard Culver
     Packy McCloud                 Fred Howard
     Mesquite Molly                Gwen Delano
     Scorpion                      Robert Griffin
     Driver                        Ted von Eltz
     Sheriff                       Malcolm McCoy
     Chief (double Driver)         Ted von Eltz

239. December 19, 1950, Tuesday    The Happy (Valley) Land
     Cast:
     Steve Adams/Straight Arrow    Howard Culver
     Packy McCloud                 Fred Howard
     Blackie (Scorpion)            Robert Griffin
     Sam Daley                     Parley Baer
     Lasker                        Tyler McVey
     Constoya                      Ted von Eltz
     Sheriff                       Ralph Moody
     Man (double)                  Ralph Moody
     Man #1                        Ted von Eltz

240. December 21, 1950, Thursday   Peace On Earth
     Cast:
     Steve Adams/Straight Arrow    Howard Culver
     Packy McCloud                 Fred Howard
     Mesquite Molly                Gwen Delano
     Chinnaberry                   Tim Graham
     Sierra                        Herb Butterfield

241.  December 26, 1950, Tuesday    King Of The River
      Cast:
      Steve Adams/Straight Arrow     Howard Culver
      Packy McCloud                  Fred Howard
      Lathan                         Tudor Owen
      Crusher                        Lou Merrill
      Denver                         Jack Moyles
      Voice (double)                 Jack Moyles

242.  December 28, 1950, Thursday   High Stakes
      Cast:
      Steve Adams/Straight Arrow     Howard Culver
      Packy McCloud                  Fred Howard
      Mesquite Molly                 Gwen Delano
      Burley                         Ken Christy
      Turk                           Vic Perrin
      Grey Wolf                      Jan Arvan
      Colonel                        Herb Rawlinson
      Allison                        Whitfield Connor

MUTAL BROADCASTING SUSTEM - 1951

243.  January 2, 1951, Tuesday       The Brand
      Cast:
      Steve Adams/Straight Arrow     Howard Culver
      Packy McCloud                  Fred Howard
      Brad                           George Neise
      Ritchie                        Olan Soulé
      Sal                            Lillian Buyeff
      Murdo                          Ed Max
      Shawnee                        Jack Kruschen
      Man                            Nestor Paiva
      Outlaw                         Nestor Paiva

244.  January 4, 1951, Thursday      The Wasteland
      Cast:
      Steve Adams/Straight Arrow     Howard Culver
      Packy McCloud                  Fred Howard
      Mesquite Molly                 Gwen Delano
      Dave                           Jonathan Hole
      Carol                          Vivi Janiss
      Slick                          Bill Bouchey
      Deever                         Wilms Herbert
      Sheriff                        Brad Brown
      Man (double)                   Brad Brown

245. January 9, 1951, Tuesday  Spur For A Rustler
   Cast:
   Steve Adams/Straight Arrow  Howard Culver
   Packy McCloud  Fred Howard
   Brawley  Lou Merrill
   Latigo  Herb Ellis
   Sheriff  Parley Baer
   Bannister  Herb Butterfield
   Man (double)  Herb Butterfield

246. January 11, 1951, Thursday  Danger Weaves A Web
   Cast:
   Steve Adams/Straight Arrow  Howard Culver
   Packy McCloud  Fred Howard
   Mesquite Molly  Gwen Delano
   Istaqua  Virginia Gregg
   Black Snake  Ralph Moody
   Roach  John Dehner
   Indian  Jan Arvan
   Driver (double)  Jan Arvan

247. January 16, 1951, Tuesday  The Glittering (Mt) Mountain
   Cast:
   Steve Adams/Straight Arrow  Howard Culver
   Packy McCloud  Fred Howard
   Tod  Sam Edwards
   Hackley  Ken Christy
   Slater  Don Diamond
   Grey Horn  Bill Green
   Man (double)

248. January 18, 1951, Thursday  Yellowleg
   Cast:
   Steve Adams/Straight Arrow  Howard Culver
   Packy McCloud  Fred Howard
   Mesquite Molly  Gwen Delano
   June  Alvina Temple
   Clay  Whit Connor
   Fargo  Jack Moyles
   Slade  Tyler McVey
   Governor  Ted von Eltz

249.  January 23, 1951, Tuesday        Backfire
      Cast:
      Steve Adams/Straight Arrow        Howard Culver
      Packy McCloud                     Fred Howard
      Clinch                            Bob Griffin
      Storm                             Tom Holland
      Scar                              Jack Kruschen
      Chief                             Ralph Moody

250.  January 25, 1951, Thursday       Make Way For Murder
      Cast:
      Steve Adams/Straight Arrow        Howard Culver
      Packy McCloud                     Fred Howard
      Mesquite Molly                    Gwen Delano
      Tami                              Byron Kane
      Maria                             Lillian Buyeff
      Turk                              Lou Merrill
      Haslip                            Tim Graham
      Man (double)                      Byron Kane
      Talon                             Bill Bouchey

251.  January 30, 1951, Tuesday        Maverick
      Cast:
      Steve Adams/Straight Arrow        Howard Culver
      Packy McCloud                     Fred Howard
      Jerry                             Eddie Firestone
      Lex                               George Neise
      Slick                             John Dehner
      Ross                              Herb Butterfield
      Sheriff                           Parley Baer
      Man 2                             Bob Bruce

252.  February 1, 1951, Thursday       Desert Glory
      Cast:
      Steve Adams/Straight Arrow        Howard Culver
      Packy McCloud                     Fred Howard
      Mesquite Molly                    Gwen Delano
      Peter                             Johnny McGovern
      Deborah                           Elizabeth Root
      Minifee                           Jonathan Hole
      Trench                            Ken Christy
      Buzz                              Joe DuVal

| 253. | February 6, 1951, Tuesday | Boundary War |
|---|---|---|
| | Cast: | |
| | Steve Adams/Straight Arrow | Howard Culver |
| | Packy McCloud | Fred Howard |
| | Pike | Ralph Moody |
| | Slade | Herb Ellis |
| | Bannerman | Lou Merrill |
| | Governor | Ralph Moody |
| | Sergeant | Ted von Eltz |
| | Chief | Ted von Eltz |
| | Colonel | Stan Waxman |
| 254. | February 8, 1951, Thursday | Double Danger |
| | Cast: | |
| | Steve Adams/Straight Arrow | Howard Culver |
| | Packy McCloud | Fred Howard |
| | Mesquite Molly | Gwen Delano |
| | Andrew | Vic Perrin |
| | Jason | Jack Moyles |
| | Scragg | Dave Young |
| | Agnes | Virginia Gregg |
| | Man | John Frank |
| | Man 2 | Vic Perrin |
| | Woman | Virginia Gregg |
| 255. | February 13, 1951, Tuesday | Path To Peril |
| | Cast: | |
| | Steve Adams/Straight Arrow | Howard Culver |
| | Packy McCloud | Fred Howard |
| | Bullock | Ed Max |
| | Sneed | Bob Griffin |
| | Chief | Bill Green |
| | Outlaw | Tim Graham |
| | Man | Earl Lee |
| | Driver | Earl Lee |
| 256. | February 15, 1951, Thursday | Trail By Night |
| | Cast: | |
| | Steve Adams/Straight Arrow | Howard Culver |
| | Packy McCloud | Fred Howard |
| | Mesquite Molly | Gwen Delano |
| | Saddler | Ken Christy |
| | Good Heart | Elmore Vincent |
| | Dakota | Tyler McVey |
| | Voice | Vic Rodman |
| | Johnson | Malcolm McCoy |
| | Man | Malcolm McCoy |

257. February 20, 1951, Tuesday    Iron Wheels
     Cast:
     Steve Adams/Straight Arrow    Howard Culver
     Packy McCloud                 Fred Howard
     Denny                         Jack Moyles
     Keller                        Joe DuVal
     Wylie                         Lou Merrill
     Trig                          George Neise
     Sturgeon                      Dave Young
     Man (double)                  George Neise

258. February 22, 1951, Thursday   Mystery Ranch
     Cast:
     Steve Adams/Straight Arrow    Howard Culver
     Packy McCloud                 Fred Howard
     Mesquite Molly                Gwen Delano
     Sally                         Connie Crowder
     Jacklin                       Sam Edwards
     Meechum                       Ralph Moody
     Sauter                        John Dehner

259. February 27, 1951, Tuesday    Corral A Killer
     Cast:
     Steve Adams/Straight Arrow    Howard Culver
     Packy McCloud                 Fred Howard
     Travis                        Ed Max
     Welch                         Nestor Paiva
     Cantrell                      Ted von Eltz

260. March 1, 1951, Thursday       Quicksand Crossing
     Cast:
     Steve Adams/Straight Arrow    Howard Culver
     Packy McCloud                 Fred Howard
     Mesquite Molly                Gwen Delano
     Carstairs                     Bob Griffin
     Denver                        Dave Young
     Sheriff                       Parley Baer
     Driver                        Malcolm McCoy
     Voice                         Malcolm McCoy

261. March 6, 1951, Tuesday        Fires Of War
     Cast:
     Steve Adams/Straight Arrow    Howard Culver
     Packy McCloud                 Fred Howard
     Riki Ton                      Johnny McGovern
     Yellow Robe                   Ralph Moody

Straight Arrow Radio Log 95

|        | Reagel                     | Bill Bouchey        |
|        | Lasher                     | Herb Ellis          |
|        | Grey Wolf                  | Jan Arvan           |

262.    March 8, 1951, Thursday     Guns For Gold
        Cast:
        Steve Adams/Straight Arrow   Howard Culver
        Packy McCloud                Fred Howard
        Mesquite Molly               Gwen Delano
        Morley                       Vic Perrin
        Lynch                        Ken Christy
        Cantwell                     Earl Lee
        Proctor                      Tim Graham
        Voice                        Vic Perrin
        Voice 2                      Earl Lee

263.    March 13, 1951, Tuesday     Medicine Man
        Cast:
        Steve Adams/Straight Arrow   Howard Culver
        Packy McCloud                Fred Howard
        Spider                       Jack Moyles
        Dirk                         Jack Carol
        Elkhorn                      Ted von Eltz
        Outlaw                       Ted von Eltz
        Indian                       Bill Green
        Indian 2                     Jack Carol

264.    March 15, 1951, Thursday    The Finger Of Manitou
        Cast:
        Steve Adams/Straight Arrow   Howard Culver
        Packy McCloud                Fred Howard
        Mesquite Molly               Gwen Delano
        Grey Coyote                  Ralph Moody
        Dawson                       John Dehner
        Krag                         Val Brown
        Voice (double)               Ralph Moody

265.    March 20, 1951, Tuesday     Track Of Murder
        Cast:
        Steve Adams/Straight Arrow   Howard Culver
        Packy McCloud                Fred Howard
        Harkins                      Herb Butterfield
        Surley                       Bob Griffin
        Spike                        Nestor Paiva
        Voice                        Herb Butterfield
        Voice 2                      Nestor Paiva

266.  March 22, 1951, Thursday         Drumbeat
      Cast:
      Steve Adams/Straight Arrow       Howard Culver
      Packy McCloud                    Fred Howard
      Mesquite Molly                   Gwen Delano
      Billy                            Jeffrey Silver
      Carl                             Whit Connor
      Sal                              Elizabeth Root
      Badger                           Bill Bouchey
      Weasel                           Charlie Calvert
      Outlaw (double)                  Whit Connor

267.  March 27, 1951, Tuesday          The Sheriff Learns The Law
      Cast:
      Steve Adams/Straight Arrow       Howard Culver
      Packy McCloud                    Fred Howard
      Talbot                           Forrest Lewis
      Blakey                           Ted von Eltz
      Crutch                           Ken Christy
      Dirk                             Tyler McVey
      Man                              John Frank

268.  March 29, 1951, Thursday         Broken Wheel
      Cast:
      Steve Adams/Straight Arrow       Howard Culver
      Packy McCloud                    Fred Howard
      Mesquite Molly                   Gwen Delano
      Frenchy                          Jan Arvan
      Bacher                           Lou Merrill
      Jenkins                          Jack Moyles
      Bart                             Malcolm McCoy
      Man                              Malcolm McCoy
      Woman                            Betty Hanna

269.  April 3, 1951, Tuesday           Feathered Arrows
      Cast:
      Steve Adams/Straight Arrow       Howard Culver
      Packy McCloud                    Fred Howard
      Logan                            Jonathan Hole
      Sergeant                         Ralph Moody
      Mablee                           Bill Green
      Cochin                           Jan Arvan
      Rackman                          Bill Bouchey
      Nails                            Brad Brown
      Deerskin (double)                Ralph Moody
      Corporal (double)                Brad Brown

270. April 5, 1951, Thursday         Deadly (Smoke) Current
     Cast:
     Steve Adams/Straight Arrow      Howard Culver
     Packy McCloud                   Fred Howard
     Mesquite Molly                  Gwen Delano
     Bull                            Ken Christy
     Breckenridge                    Frances X. Bushman
     Snag                            Jack Carol
     Indian                          Ted von Eltz
     Outlaw                          Ted von Eltz

271. April 10, 1951, Tuesday         Flash In The Pan
     Cast:
     Steve Adams/Straight Arrow      Howard Culver
     Packy McCloud                   Fred Howard
     Mesquite Molly                  Gwen Delano
     Rufus                           Herb Butterfield
     Dade                            Johnny McGovern
     Rollins                         Ed Max
     Snipe                           George Neise
     Sheriff                         Tim Graham

272. April 12, 1951, Thursday        False Rider
     Cast:
     Steve Adams/Straight Arrow      Howard Culver
     Packy McCloud                   Fred Howard
     Shattuck                        Whit Connor
     Naylin                          Bob Griffin
     Smokey                          Forrest Lewis
     Sheriff                         Parley Baer
     Ma                              Marian Richman
     Digger (double)                 Forrest Lewis
     Women (double)                  Marian Richman

273. April 17, 1951, Tuesday         Two Tribes West
     Cast:
     Steve Adams/Straight Arrow      Howard Culver
     Packy McCloud                   Fred Howard
     Doniger                         Jack Moyles
     Speer                           Nestor Paiva
     Eagle Claw                      Jan Arvan
     Jacanda                         Ralph Moody
     Spotted Heron                   Bill Green
     Indian (double)                 Jan Arvan

274. April 19, 1951, Thursday    Calico
Cast:
Steve Adams/Straight Arrow    Howard Culver
Packy McCloud    Fred Howard
Mesquite Molly    Gwen Delano
Kelso    Ken Christy
Lockwood    Herb Vigran
Dallas    Tyler McVey
Randall    Earl Lee
Voice 1    Malcolm McCoy

275. April 24, 1951, Tuesday    Under Suspicion
Cast:
Steve Adams/Straight Arrow    Howard Culver
Packy McCloud    Fred Howard
Jeff    Bob Bruce'
Chuck    George Neise
Fargo    Bill Bouchey
Winters    Ted von Eltz
Sheriff    Val Brown
Jenson    Ted von Eltz
Voice    Val Brown

276. April 26, 1951, Thursday    The Misfit
Cast:
Steve Adams/Straight Arrow    Howard Culver
Packy McCloud    Fred Howard
Mesquite Molly    Gwen Delano
Clem    Sam Edwards
Penny    Alvina Temple
Sanders    Herb Butterfield
Man    Brad Brown
Woman    Connie Crowder

277. May 1, 1951, Tuesday    The Dry Earth
Cast:
Steve Adams/Straight Arrow    Howard Culver
Packy McCloud    Fred Howard
Mesquite Molly    Gwen Delano
Cash    Forrest Lewis
Riker    Ralph Moody
Langley    Jack Carol
Woman    Lillian Buyeff
Secoya    Jan Arvan
Squaw    Lillian Buyeff
Indian    Ralph Moody

278. May 3, 1951, Thursday  Spread Eagle
Cast:
Steve Adams/Straight Arrow  Howard Culver
Packy McCloud  Fred Howard
Parker  Parley Baer
Sarah  Virginia Gregg
Dirk  Jack Moyles
Montana  Charlie Calvert
Man  Parley Baer
Woman  Virginia Gregg

279. May 8, 1951, Tuesday  Trail's End
Cast:
Steve Adams/Straight Arrow  Howard Culver
Packy McCloud  Fred Howard
Mesquite Molly  Gwen Delano
Judy  Janet Stewart
Paul  Eddie Firestone
Lobo  Ken Christy
Clem  Nestor Paiva
Jared  Leo Cleary
Shortell  Leo Cleary
Latigo  Nestor Paiva
Boy (in commercial)  Stuffy Singer
Man (in commercial)  Bill Green

280. May 10, 1951, Thursday  Reverse Proof
Cast:
Steve Adams/Straight Arrow  Howard Culver
Packy McCloud  Fred Howard
Sam  Junius Matthews
Leach  Bill Bouchey
Krell  Tyler McVey
Sheriff  Tim Graham
Slater (double)  John Frank
Driver  John Frank

281. May 15, 1951, Tuesday  Rustler's Run
Cast:
Steve Adams/Straight Arrow  Howard Culver
Packy McCloud  Fred Howard
Mesquite Molly  Gwen Delano
Pollock  Tudor Owen
Ben  Whit Connor
Forrest ~~Cantrell~~  Bob Griffin
Slaughter  Frank Gerstle
Voice (double)  Whit Connor
Man (in commercial)  Joe Granby
Boy (in commercial)  David DuVal

282. May 17, 1951, Thursday     The Dark Cave
Cast:
| Steve Adams/Straight Arrow | Howard Culver |
|---|---|
| Packy McCloud | Fred Howard |
| Preston | Olan Soulé |
| Buffalo Horn ~~Long Bow~~ | Ted von Eltz |
| Medicine Man | Ralph Moody |
| Black Flint | Eddie Fields |
| Bledsoe | Dave Young |
| Colonel | Ralph Moody |
| Voice | Eddie Fields |

283. May 22, 1951, Tuesday     Gamble For Gain
Cast:
| Steve Adams/Straight Arrow | Howard Culver |
|---|---|
| Packy McCloud | Fred Howard |
| Koster | George Neise |
| Roach | Jack Moyles |
| Granger | Herb Butterfield |
| Spider | Bob Bruce |
| Man | Bob Bruce |
| Voice | Herb Butterfield |

284. May 24, 1951, Thursday     The Conspirator
Cast:
| Steve Adams/Straight Arrow | Howard Culver |
|---|---|
| Packy McCloud | Fred Howard |
| Mesquite Molly | Gwen Delano |
| Isabel | Marian Richman |
| Carlos | Tony Barrett |
| Savage | Lou Merrill |
| Ranney | Jesse Kirkpatrick |
| Commandant | Forrest Lewis |
| Voice | Forrest Lewis |

285. May 29, 1951, Tuesday     Whiphand
Cast:
| Steve Adams/Straight Arrow | Howard Culver |
|---|---|
| Packy McCloud | Fred Howard |
| Mesquite Molly | Gwen Delano |
| Whip | Ken Christy |
| Johnny | Sam Edwards |
| Shiloh | Nestor Paiva |
| Sheriff | Tim Graham |
| Indian (double) | Nestor Paiva |

|  |  |  |
|---|---|---|
|  | Voice (double) | Sam Edwards |
|  | Man (in commercial) | Joe Granby |
|  | Boy (in commercial) | David DuVal |

286. May 31, 1951, Thursday — The Bitter Wind
Cast:
| | |
|---|---|
| Steve Adams/Straight Arrow | Howard Culver |
| Packy McCloud | Fred Howard |
| Gahnway | Eddie Fields |
| Madanka | Ralph Moody |
| Chadwick | Jonathan Hole |
| Mary | Virginia Gregg |

287. June 5, 1951, Tuesday — Rainbow's End
Cast:
| | |
|---|---|
| Steve Adams/Straight Arrow | Howard Culver |
| Packy McCloud | Fred Howard |
| Mesquite Molly | Gwen Delano |
| Spurlock | Bob Griffin |
| Yancey | Tyler McVey |
| Duncan | Tudor Owen |
| Woman | Lillian Buyeff |
| Man | Leo Cleary |
| Man 2 | Tyler McVey |
| Woman 2 | Lillian Buyeff |
| Man (in commercial) | Joe Granby |
| Boy (in commercial) | David DuVal |

288. June 7, 1951, Thursday — Eagle Claw
Cast: No additional information available

289. June 12, 1951, Tuesday — Owlhoot
Cast:
| | |
|---|---|
| Steve Adams/Straight Arrow | Howard Culver |
| Packy McCloud | Fred Howard |
| Mesquite Molly | Gwen Delano |
| Carabou | Jack Moyles |
| Ranny | Bob Bruce |
| Running Bear | Ted von Eltz |
| Squaw | Virginia Gregg |
| Nicolette | Herb Butterfield |
| Man (in commercial) | Joe Granby |
| Boy (in commercial) | David DuVal |

| | | |
|---|---|---|
| 290. | June 14, 1951, Thursday | Blanket Indian |
| | Cast: | |
| | Steve Adams/Straight Arrow | Howard Culver |
| | Packy McCloud | Fred Howard |
| | Spotted Curlew | Jan Arvan |
| | Grey Owl (double) | John Dehner |
| | Tomahawk | Bill Green |
| | Burley | John Dehner |
| | Ringo | Ralph Moody |
| | Indian (double) | Ralph Moody |
| 291. | June 19, 1951, Tuesday | Flood Tide |
| | Cast: | |
| | Steve Adams/Straight Arrow | Howard Culver |
| | Packy McCloud | Fred Howard |
| | Snider | Ken Christy |
| | Petrov | Nestor Paiva |
| | Indian | Eddie Fields |
| | Yipano | Vic Perrin |
| | Man (double) | Vic Perrin |
| | Man 2 (double) | Eddie Fields |
| 292. | June 21, 1951, Thursday | The Long Summer |
| | Cast: | |
| | Steve Adams/Straight Arrow | Howard Culver |
| | Packy McCloud | Fred Howard |
| | Mesquite Molly | Gwen Delano |
| | Rogey | Stuffy Singer |
| | Abby | Florida Edwards |
| | Catlett | Parley Baer |
| | Racklin | Bill Bouchey |
| | Two Claws | Ralph Moody |
| | Faro (double) | Parley Baer |

## NOTES

1. In this story, The Iron Horse, Straight Arrow's golden palomino received the name "Fury," which was selected from 50,000 submissions. The Iron Horse was originally scheduled for July 15, 1948, but was switched with Oasis In The Desert.

2. There were 39 shows aired over the California-based Don Lee Network. In 1936, the ten Don Lee stations and the thirteen Colonial Network stations on the east coast joined Mutual Broadcasting System to form the third coast-to-coast network.

KHJ, formed in 1922, was the key station of what was in 1948 the largest regional network.

3. The first show aired over nationwide Mutual radio, Roaring Rivers, has the same title as the second story in Magazine Enterprise's Straight Arrow comic #1.

4. This is the same title for the special Straight Arrow broadcast on September 18, 1949 (see footnote # 7).

5. Land Of Our Fathers made-up one side of the 1974 Mark 56 Straight Arrow recording as well as the basis for the story by the same title published as the second entry in Straight Arrow comic #2.

6. Sponsor magazine credited the poor response to the third premium offer, Straight Arrow Tie Clip, for Nabisco's decision to interrupt sponsorship for 13 weeks. Straight Arrow remained on Mutual as a sustainer one day a week until Nabisco resumed sponsorship in September, 1949.

7. This Special Broadcast aired September 18 had no script number notation and has the same title and list of characters as the Buffalo Hunt aired February 10, 1949. However, the casting is different. This special Sunday episode was presented five days prior to the Mutual special show, "The Song of the Tom-tom" a salute to the American Indian airing on American Indian Day, Friday, September 23, 1949 (9 - 9:30 p.m. EDST), which included many stars as well as Ted Robertson and Ray Kemper from the production staff of Straight Arrow.

8. In researching the scripts we discovered that there was not a number 172; however, the numbering continued as if there had been! The "special" September 18, 1949 show also had no number as well, thus the count for the shows aired is correct at 292.

9. The last show, Long Summer, rounded out 253 shows over the Mutual nationwide system. This figure includes the Sunday "special," September 18, 1949, and the four repeat shows during September, 1950. This combined with the 39 shows over the Don Lee Network totals 292. Stark wrote a total of 288 scripts plus the audition for a total of 289. This Straight Arrow radio log is as near complete as possible after examining nearly every

script cover sheet from Nabisco archives and comparing them to Stark's "ledger," which is extremely reliable as it was used for financial and tax purposes. The notations in parentheses are the working titles from Stark.

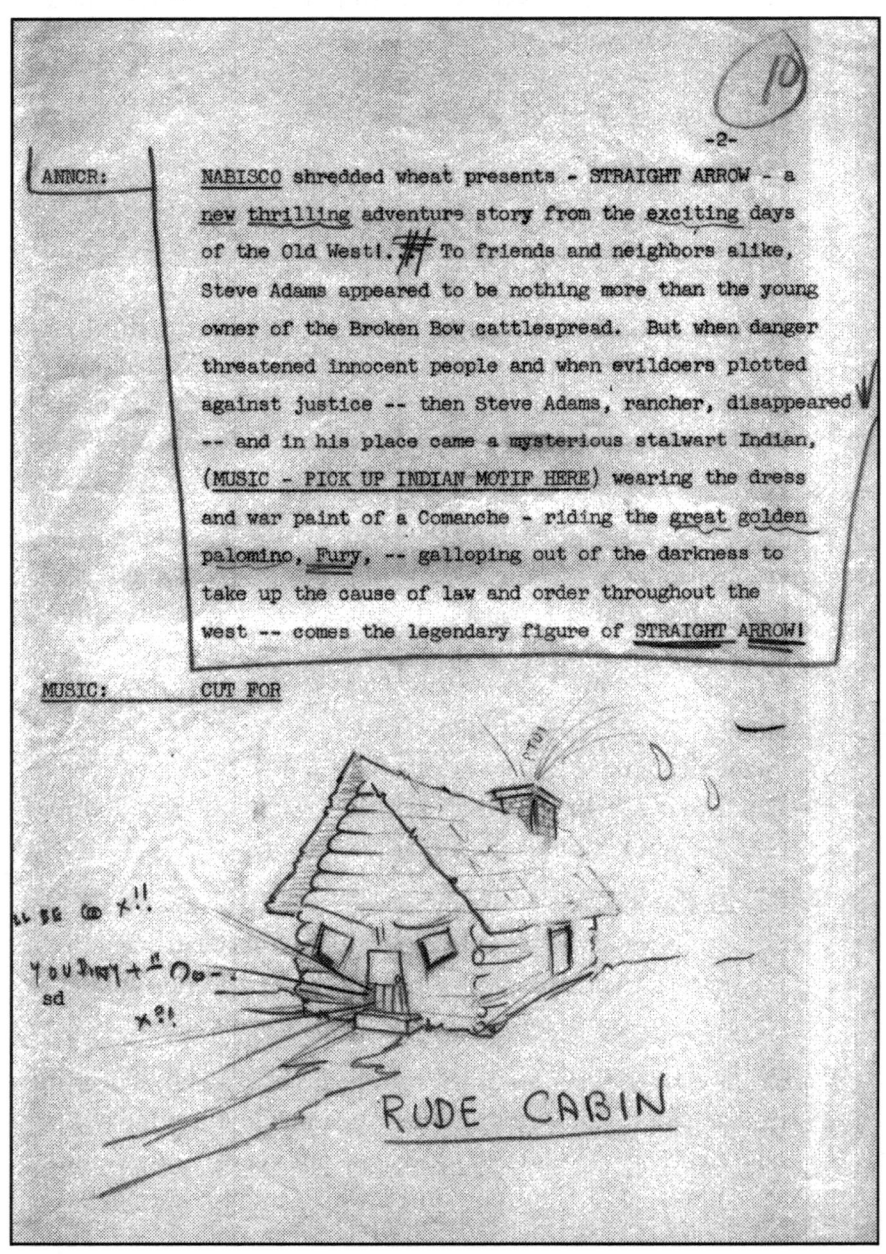

Sketch by Frank Bingman.

# Getting It Right?

Who was Straight Arrow and who was Steve Adams?

Straight Arrow and Steve Adams were introduced to radio listeners in the premiere production on May 6, 1948, by the announcer with "To friend and neighbors alike, Steve Adams appeared to be nothing more than the young owner of the Broken Bow cattle spread. But when danger threatened innocent people and when evildoers plotted against justice—then Steve Adams, rancher, disappeared—and in his place came a mysterious stalwart Indian..."

This same introduction would appear in the first issue of Magazine Enterprises *Straight Arrow* comic with a February/March 1950 dateline. The dual identity was defined, but not clear as who is who! A *Hollywood Citizen News* article dated May 6, 1948, states; "Howard

Culver is Steve Adams, a young rancher, who assumes the character and appearance of a young Comanche Indian..." In the *Los Angeles Daily News*, January 28, 1949 an article proclaims "Culver plays the dual role of Steve Adams, rancher and solid citizen, who has the strange power of becoming "Straight Arrow," a fabulous Comanche warrior..." Interestingly John Dunning's *Tune in Yesterday* (Prentice Hall, 1976) and *On The Air* (Oxford University Press, 1998) refers to the deep resonant change of Steve Adams voice when he donned the outfit of a Comanche warrior to ride from the cave as Straight Arrow to Clark Kent assuming his identity of Superman. However in several newspaper articles the comparisons have more to do with the question of alter egos, or as one reporter wrote, "a superman in chaps." Superman was understood to be in disguise when he was Clark Kent and the same should have been apparent for Straight Arrow in disguise as Steve Adams. It was never Steve Adams riding to the secret cave to become Straight Arrow, but Straight Arrow, after righting the wrong, becoming Steve Adams.

In Bill Owens and Frank Buxton's book, *Radio's Golden Age* (Easton Valley Press 1966), the identity of Straight Arrow read, "Indian born Steve Adams, the owner of Broken Bow ranch, donned Comanche war paint and became Straight Arrow..." On a second read how equivocal this line, but printed on the inside cover of the Injun-uity Manual is a story titled "The Cave of Gold (How Steve Adams became Straight Arrow)." This story was penned by Sheldon Stark, writer of all the Straight Arrow radio scripts, and condensed from a more elaborated narration. It is a simple story of Steve Adams, who while stalking a beautiful palomino, rescues a stranger (Packy McCloud) from a group of outlaws that were stirring up the Indians. The palomino appeared to be beckoning Steve Adams to follow. When Adams, with the wounded Packy, follow the horse they discover a secret cave - a cave of gold! Once in the cave out of harm's way, the palomino and the gold causes Packy to recall an old Indian legend of a mysterious Indian, taller and stronger and braver than others, riding a golden horse, shooting a golden arrow and saving the Indians. Steve then showed Packy a golden arrowhead he wore around his neck, telling him how Steve had been born Comanche, orphaned and found and raised by white ranchers. So here is the material of legends; Steve Adams is certainly an Indian, but the transformation that takes place in the secret cave of gold when Steve Adams dresses in the outfit and puts on the war paint of an Indian and rides out of the cave as "Straight Arrow" on the trail of justice, is shrouded in mystery.

John Dunning's *Tune in Yesterday* (Prentice Hall, 1976) had it wrong; Steve Adams simply disguises himself as Straight Arrow and rides. Dunning would correct this, in his, *On The Air* (Oxford University Press 1998). In the magazine *Under Western Skies* (Issue #10, May 1980, p. 51) Paul Dellinger wrote "...Straight Arrow was not really a Comanche as he appeared". Denis Gifford, a recognized comic book authority, describes the Straight Arrow in his book *The International Book of Comics* 1984 (p. 94) "...this clarity of speech was not an honorable attempt to restore dignity to the first Americans. It is because Straight Arrow was really white man Steve Adams...". In the book *Handbook of Old Time Radio* (1993) by Jon Swartz and Robert Reinehr Steve Adams is described as a young rancher raised among the Comanches and finally Gerald Nachman's *Raised On Radio* (Pantheon Books 1998) listed Straight Arrow as a favorite, but then went on to write "...Straight Arrow, whose hero was, in fact, not an Indian at all but Steve Adams, a white cattle rancher in red face." A couple of others who got it wrong were Gary Yoggy in his *When Radio Wore Spurs* (1984) and Ron Lackmann in his *Same Time, Same Station* (1996).

Since the introduction of the Straight Arrow newsletter *Pow-Wow* (Fall 1986- Pow-Wow presents the Fred L. Meagher Special Winter 2001/2002 -partially in *AlterEgo* #11 November 2001) the internet sites have had it right. Jack French, member of the Metro Washington (DC) Old time Radio Club and editor of the club's newsletter, *Radio Recall*, made a special effort to get it right in his internet article "Straight Arrow."

It was Straight Arrow that rode, in his disguise as Steve Adams, to Sundown Valley and the secret cave. Donning Indian garb, war paint and riding out of the cave with his war cry, "Kaneewah, Fury" echoing, Straight Arrow rode bareback on his great golden palomino.

# Straight Arrow In Person

On February 7, 1949, when Straight Arrow rode into millions of American homes at 8:00 p.m. on Monday evening, over the 409 stations of the nationwide Mutual Broadcasting System, the program had run 39 weeks over the Don Lee Network, a loosely connected group of stations on the West Coast, affiliated with Mutual. There was an 18-episodes trial run which was extended 21 weeks, due to the tremendous response to the show and a berth over the nationwide Mutual hook-up. The original premiere production at 8:00 p.m. on Thursday, May 6, 1948, produced in the studios of KHJ - Hollywood, was only the beginning of a clever multi-media promotion that was well-tuned by the nationwide airing in February, 1949.

One of the preliminary introductions of Straight Arrow to the nation was Mutual's Hitching Post production, hosted by Ben Alexander (Jack Webbs' early partner on TV's Dragnet). Among the screaming mob of youngsters, western stars from the Silver Screen lent their talent and praises for Straight Arrow. The Hitching Post, a popular theater for watching cowboy movies, presented the coronation of Little Chief Straight Arrow and Little Princess Straight Arrow. But no appearance was made by Straight Arrow or any other of the main characters. Apparently from the beginning, there had been a cooperative decision not to present Straight Arrow in person. However in 1951 the Portland, Oregon, Rose Parade Committee requested that Straight Arrow/Steve Adams ride as Parade Marshal of the Junior Rose Parade. Lois Culver, Howard Culver's widow, does not recall who initiated the request, nor where it was originally directed. She supposed that the invitation passed from Portland to KHJ to McCann-Erickson-Los Angeles to Nabisco in New York City. Whatever the direction, Mrs. Culver recalled that the answer was an emphatic "no!" Later Nabisco recanted, and permission was extended for Howard Culver to participate in the parade as Straight Arrow. Culver was basically on his own, as there was no financial or promotional support from Nabisco Headquarters. The letters between the chairman of the Junior Rose Parade Committee and Culver do indicate that Nabisco in Portland was supportive, as well as, of course, the Parade Committee, which offset the expenses for Howard and Lois Culver to attend. Culver was quite excited about having the opportunity to play his radio character "live." "Howard was always for doing the new and different," Mrs. Culver recalled. The correspondence between Portland and Culver also revealed Howard's only apprehension was that the horse he rode be parade-trained.

The Rose Parade was scheduled for June 9, 1951. The Culvers arrived in Portland the evening of June 7. As the plane prepared to land in Portland, Culver changed into his rented Indian costume and put on Indian topaz jewelry, a gift from Mrs. Culver. Mrs. Culver remembered that, as Culver peered through the plane window to a waiting crowd of adults and youngsters, many dressed as Indians, he had pangs of nervousness. He exited the airplane in full Straight Arrow regalia to a cheering crowd madeup of Parade officials, the Press, the Junior Rose Festival's Queen and Junior Prime Ministers of the Junior Rose Parade. According to Mrs. Culver, Culver was visibly flustered, and his welcoming "How" created more tension when he was answered with a volley of "Hows" from the waiting young Indians. The photographs of Culver at the airport show a very stoic Indian, holding himself taut in an attempt to display muscular arms as well to add height to his 5' 8" frame. Throughout the days in Portland, Mrs. Culver recorded the events on 16mm colored film, which was later edited into a seven-minute movie. The film shows a much more relaxed Culver enjoying his role as Straight Arrow, signing autographs, chatting with the youngsters and gamely managing "Fury."

The appointed horse was a beautiful Palomino, a credit to Straight Arrow's radio Fury, but it was not the parade-trained horse Culver hoped for - in fact, Mrs. Culver said that it was the first time the horse had been in a parade. From a cream-colored convertible following Straight Arrow and Fury, Mrs. Culver recorded a very confident Culver handling the horse with the skill of a trained rider and, true to form, there were no stirrups! Straight Arrow rode the streets of Portland bareback. Years later, Culver told SPERDVAC that the horse had a chafed mouth at the parade's end, due to Culver's efforts to control it. In the Portland Rose Parade scrapbook, there is a slightly out-of-focus photograph of Culver looking pensive.

The 16mm film opens with shots of King Tower, the hotel where the Culvers were housed as guests of the Rose Parade. A sleek maroon Buick was made available to the Culvers and contrasted sharply with the fully costumed Straight Arrow as he waved and entered the car. The film also reveals that Culver was extremely conscious of his appearance as Straight Arrow. Judicious use of the various costume items created an Indian that could easily satisfy any youngster's imagined Straight Arrow. A newspaper clip told of a near catastrophe when a maid at the King Tower misplaced the sponge used to apply body make-up to Culver, giving his skin the Indian hue. After a frantic search, Culver gave up and was forced to use his fingers for the make-up.

There is no doubt that Straight Arrow was the "hit" that Rose Parade officials anticipated when the invitation was extended. Newspapers reported that the combination of excellent weather and "Straight Arrow" made the 1951 parade the best attended to that date, with over 100,000 spectators and 10,000 children covering a 20-block route to view the two hour-long procession. There were reports of "record crowds" and "howling youngsters" in article after article in various Portland newspa-

Douglas Purdy (L), Prime Minister to the 1951 Junior Rose Queen, Donna Lee Howe, smiles at the camera as Queen Donna presents roses to Mrs. Howard (Lois) Culver and a very stoic and pensive Straight Arrow (Howard Culver) on their arrival at the airport in Portland Oregon on June 7, 1951.

pers. It was also reported in the newspaper that the unannounced appearance of Straight Arrow at the rose bush planting ceremony in Peninsular Park brought screams of delight from the surprised youngsters, and even the "older generation" stopped eating their picnic lunches to take a brief look at Straight Arrow. Culver was "knighted" with the presentation of the Junior Rose Festival's Medallion of Honor.

One added concession for Culver's appearance was the use of the car to travel to Longview, Oregon, to spend two days visiting Mrs. Culver's parents, Mr. and Mrs. E. E. Hayes. The Longview newspapers also gave space to Straight Arrow's visit and Culver appears in the 16mm film dressed in full Indian outfit signing autographs from a chaise longue in the Hayes' yard. Culver, in his SPERDVAC talk, indicated that he thoroughly enjoyed acting out the role of Straight Arrow on the streets of Portland.

A seven minute video in VHS format of "Straight Arrow" in the Rose Parade is available from *Pow-Wow* see address on page 163.

## Straight Arrow In Person 113

Junior Rose Queen Donna Lee Howe receives an autograph from Straight Arrow (Howard Culver) at the Portland Rose Parade, June 9, 1951.

Straight Arrow (Howard Culver) is greeted at the Portland, Oregon airport by a gathering of young and old "Indians."

# Premiums and Merchandise and Others

When Straight Arrow went nationwide over the Mutual Broadcasting System, on February 7, 1949, a well orchestrated promotion began. There were 409 stations airing Straight Arrow and according to *Sponsor* magazine (December 19, 1949), the Nabisco nationwide sales organization, headed by 28 district sales managers in key cities and 241 agencies or branches across the nation went into action "to make Straight Arrow hit the sales bull's eye at which Nabisco is shooting." And the market Nabisco was aiming at is reflected in the broadcast times, Tuesday and Thursday at 5:00 p.m. and Monday at 8:00 p.m. Nabisco wanted the youngsters, but also aimed at an adult market. Nabisco created a bureau called Straight Arrow Enterprises to control the licensing rights. One of the first to take advantage of these rights was John Walworth, who was already familiar to Nabisco as he had created Lionel train premiums as cardboard dividers in Nabisco Shredded Wheat. Walworth said, "we would just toss out ideas at them for premiums. I don't ever recall they ever rejected any of them." The Straight Arrow premiums designed by Walworth for Nabisco were: a red feather head band, a signal drum, a bandanna and gold plated ring slide, a tribal patch and a mystic wrist kit. In an effort to cash in on the promotional investment by Nabisco, Advertisers Service Division (ASD) was created by John Walworth and Bob Weil to procure licensing rights to produce Straight Arrow merchandise items.

**PREMIUMS**

Straight Arrow rode into radio history on May 6, 1948 over the Don Lee Network on a horse with no name. Beginning with the first show, a call was made for a name. Contestants were urged to send in a name entry for Straight Arrow's horse, along with a Nabisco Shredded Wheat box top. The prize was to be a golden palomino pony "just like Straight Arrow rides" with saddle and tack or $1,000. From the 50,000 names submitted "Fury" was selected. Every entry received the first premium:

**1. Two Red Feather Head Band. (1948)**

There were two types of headbands offered. The first type offered had a band completely made of colorfully designed cardboard that was slotted at measured increments for head size adjustments and two dyed turkey feathers. The cardboard band had "Straight Arrow" in blue with a red arrow behind the name; between the two words was a blue circle with the profile of the head of a "severe" looking Indian in the center wearing two red feathers. The headband was hinged at the center with a metal grommet allowing it to be folded in half. The background was yellow with "Nabisco Shredded Wheat" written in red and a red Nabisco logo with a mention of "on your Mutual Station." The other headband had a colorfully designed cardboard band (exactly as described above), except that it had an elastic strap for adjustment, and the width was increased and the length lessened, and two dyed red turkey feathers. Included with the headband was a card measuring 13¾" x 3" that included a detachable membership (2¼" x 3") card to the Straight Arrow Tribe signed by Straight Arrow. The main body of the card was divided in half vertically with Indian sign language printed on one side and Indian trail signs on the other. There have been two different colors, orange and a pale green, identified. This second headband was offered when Straight Arrow

Premiums and Merchandise and Others 117

went nationwide February, 1949, for one box top from Nabisco Shredded Wheat. This time over 500,000 were given away. *Sponsor* magazine noted that the pony, saddle and tack were turned down in favor of the $1,000.

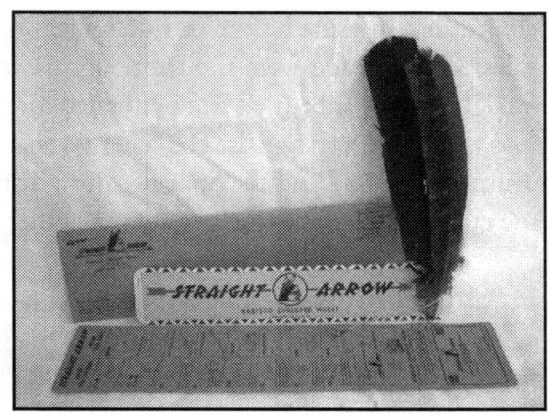

The first self-liquidating premium was a small:

**2. Straight Arrow War Drum and Secret War Drum Signals (1949)**

This premium—an Indian War Drum, drum stick and card—was available for one box-top and 25¢. The drum measured 5" in diameter and was made of thick ¼" cardboard with a paper covering giving the drum the appearance of being made of wood. It had a thin rubber top held in place by an adjustable 1" wide circular cardboard strip with "Straight Arrow" in blue, a red arrow and a red circle between the two words around a profile of the face of an Indian with two red feathers (this same motif was duplicated with a band on the bottom). A red, yellow and blue woven fabric rope was slipped through the bottom band and looped so it could be slipped over the wrist, as it was depicted in May 26, 1949 (#87) show titled "Blood Brothers":

"ARROW: Around my wrist on a rawhide thong? The war drum, Packy."

It is known that the war drum was promoted in the Straight Arrow radio script for May 16, 17, 23 and 26, 1949 (these scripts were from Sheldon

Starks' collection and did not have commercials). The single wooden drumstick had an enlarged round wooden ball painted red that was covered with thin rubber secured at the base of the ball. Printed on the stick in blue was "Straight Arrow War Drum" and "© N.B.C." A card was included that measured 12½" x 3¼" folded in half and was printed on both sides. On one side were the tribal signals and a membership card to the Straight Arrow Tribe (that was perforated for easy removal) and on the other fold were war drum signals. The other side had suggestions on how to use the drum on one fold and the Straight Arrow Tribe Council Song with the beat measure printed under each line on the other fold:

Straight Arrow is Chief
• •• • •

And I am his brave
• • • •

We all have entrance
• • • • •

To his secret cave
• • • • •

When 'er there is trouble
• • • • • •

We all ride out
• • • •

As Straight Arrow's braves
• • • • •

With our tribal shout
• • •• •

Kaneewah Fury
• • • • •

### 3. Golden Arrow Gold-Colored Arrow Clip (1949 & 1950)

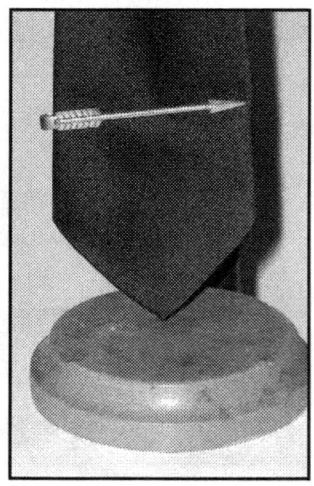

This 2¾" clip, promoted as "Straight Arrow's own symbol" with the ad copy reading "An exact copy of the golden arrow that Straight Arrow leaves everywhere he goes!" was offered as a tie clip or money clip for a youngster or adult. It was suggested that girls, young and old, could use it as a hair barrette or an ornament for a dress or scarf. Available for a Nabisco Shredded Wheat box-top and 15¢, a golden arrow had been used in ME's *Straight*

*Arrow* #1 as well as in the radio plays. However the response was so poor that, according to *Sponsor* magazine (1949), Nabisco interrupted sponsorship and Straight Arrow remained on Mutual one day a week as a sustainer for 13 weeks, June 20 (#97) until Nabisco resumed sponsorship on September 12 1949 (#109). During this period the golden arrow was promoted on the radio show. In the July 4, 1949 (#99) show, "Free and Equal," there is dialogue between Mesquite Molly and Packy re-

garding a small golden arrow left by Straight Arrow; "It's a tiny gold arrow—the mark of Straight Arrow." The infamous clip apparently was offered again in late 1950. An ad appeared on the back cover of ME *Straight Arrow* #5 (September) and was used in an October 31, 1950 (#225) script, "Avalanche."

### 4. Bandanna and Gold Plated Slide (1949)

Collectors have disputed whether the Bandanna and Gold Plated Slide was a merchandise item or a premium. John Walworth, the creator, did not recall it being offered as a premium; however, the Bandanna and Gold Plated Slide appears in a commercial in the script copy for November 24, 1949 (#139), The Deacon of Deadwood. The slide is described as a ring in the commercial, as it was in the dialogue for November 8, 1950 show, The Brother (#132); however, it was not adjustable and thus would make a poor ring for many youngsters. The approximately 19" square bandanna is red with Straight Arrow shown in opposite corners, one

with him on Fury shouting "Kaneewah Fury…" and the other, a head shot with the words "Straight Arrow" and an arrow printed in white over the head of Straight Arrow. The other two corners have Packy and Steve Adams with their names printed in white under their chins. There are drawings of moccasins, a war hatchet and a large drum and knocker clustered in the center. The only colors used are red, black, white and blue with "© 1949 National Biscuit Co." printed down one side. The gold-plated slide is a plastic ring with a small rectangular box with "Straight" on one side and "Arrow" on the opposite and an arrow in relief on the top. The diameter of the slide is ¾" and the small arrow measures 5/8". The bandanna and slide were available together for 20¢ and a box top.

## 5. Straight Arrow Good Luck Ring (Face Ring with the Secret Message, 1950)

1950 opened with the Face Ring written into the scripts for January 17 (#162) and 23 (#163) and may have begun in the January 16 (#161) story titled "The Ring." This bronze adjustable ring has a well-defined relief of Straight Arrow depicted on the broad sweep of the ring with an arrow feather etched before the word "Straight" on one side of the ring leading to the profile and on the other side, leading from the profile the word "Arrow" followed by an etched arrow head. Engraved on the inside of the ring were two secret words, "T'okah" (on the ring it reads "TOKA") meaning "foe" and "K'ahgay" (on the ring as "KAGE") meaning "friend." The words were revealed in the January 23 script as a means to locate a treasure. This series of stories started with "The Ring" January 16 and apparently ended on February 7, with "Sands of Gold." The ring required a Nabisco Shredded Wheat box top and 10¢. Youngsters were encouraged to start a Straight Arrow club with the ring as the point of interest.

### 6. Mystical Wrist Kit (1950)

Perhaps one of the most intriguing premiums was this plastic wrist kit. This 1950 premium was available for 20¢ and a box-top and included four different items. The kit had a slightly adjustable bracelet. Connected to top of the bracelet was a round removable case 1½" in diameter and ½" deep with the word " Kwa'yo" (meaning "hawk") on the bottom. The screw-on top had the words "Straight Arrow," a curved arrow and Straight Arrow's profile molded in the plastic. Inside the case was an arrowhead (1" long) with the words "Straight" on one side and "Arrow" on the other and a small hole near the base and a cowry shell (¾" long) with a small loop. A special booklet was advertised telling the history of the cowry shell as "Indian Wampum." Originally the promotion described the shell as a "genuine cowry shell"; in the ads, however it read simply "shell." John Walworth, creator of the mystic wrist kit, remembered that the Food and Drug Administration (FDA) objected. Walworth never knew the exact reason for the objection, but thought it may have had to do with the actual shell being considered of "poisonous quality." Also postal regulations at the time prohibited sending a "genuine" shell through the mail. Sheldon Stark was sent a dummy lay-up and data sheet to enable him to use the premium in the script. The kit is known to have been used in the continuing episodes between April 20 and May 18, 1950, beginning with "The Wampum" (#192) April 20, 1950. Ads appeared on the back cover of ME *Straight Arrow* #3 as well as in DC's *Detective Comics* preceding a Pow-Wow Smith story. The Mystic Wrist Kit, a favorite among collectors, is hard to find intact because the box with its removable top cover and the shell and arrowhead were loose inside.

## 7. Tribal Patch (1950)

From Navaho sand pictures to a cloth patch the Straight Arrow Tribal Patch was woven into the story lines of a Straight Arrow radio adventure following the 1950 summer break of repeat shows. In the September 26, 1950 (#215), "Deserter" production, Running Deer, a Navaho accused of deserting the Cavalry as a trail guide, leaves colorful Navaho sand pictures showing Straight Arrow's face, a gold arrow and his name as a message. Later, Straight Arrow having been captured and held prisoner with Running Bear, listens as Running Deer imagines the sand picture being made into a cloth patch. The scripts on file are from Sheldon Stark's collection and do not have commercials, but they would certainly have encouraged listeners to send a Nabisco Shredded Wheat box and 10¢ for this 3" diameter cloth patch. The patch, advertised as being made of "washable twill" and "sewn with thousands of embroidered stitches," had a blue background with an arrow in gold cloth curved over a profile of Straight Arrow in red, gold and blue. The name "Straight Arrow" is embroidered in gold and curved under the profile. A red embroidered circle frames the patch. The patch was in the script for October 3, 1950 (#217), and was hinted at in the October 5, 1950 (#218), "Pay Master." The November 1950 issue of ME *Straight Arrow* #7 had a full page ad for it on the last page of the comic as did DC *Gang Busters* #19, Dec/Jan (1950/1951).

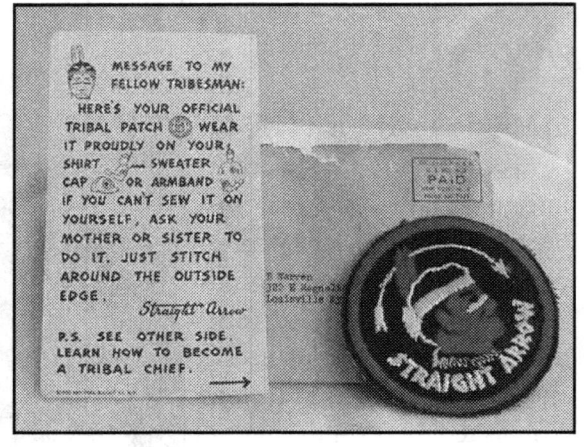

## 8. Gold Nugget Picture Ring (1950)

"See yourself in Straight Arrow's secret cave!" proclaim ads for the Gold Nugget Picture Ring. The premium, available for a Nabisco Shredded Wheat box top and 25¢ (and "your" photograph), measured ¾" diameter, was "gold dipped," and could expand slightly to fit various finger sizes. On the two side bands, "arrows" were molded and on the top of the ring there was what appears to be a gold nugget (½") on a base with the words "Straight" and "Arrow" engraved on each side, which may have been the "secret words" mentioned in the advertisements. The nugget had small circular openings on both sides. On the side with "Straight" was a lens, and on the other side was a small circular metal spring loop for holding the photographic slide of Fury, Straight Arrow and "you" in place. The picture of Straight Arrow and Fury were

artwork and the picture of "you" was from a photograph sent with your coupon, money and box top. The photograph was promised to be returned undamaged! It was the only premium that had a timeframe listed: "Allow at least 3 weeks for delivery." The golden nugget ring was referred to in the episode of December 7, 1950 (#236), but only as a guide to a treasure, which was not discovered in this particular story. The same characters were portrayed in December 12, 14 and 19, 1950 (#237, #238 and #239), which would indicate that the golden nugget might have figured in the story line. The ring was advertised on the back cover of ME *Straight Arrow* #9 (January 1951). In 1987, through the efforts of the Fugates (Gary and Charlotte), the golden nugget ring offer was renewed. *Pow-Wow* (Vol.1 #3, Fall 1987) announced the offer to the membership's attention. Charlotte, an artist, created the art work of Straight Arrow and Fury based on the delineation displayed in the golden nugget ad. Gary worked out the problem of making a photographic slide of the drawing and a snapshot to put "you" in the secret cave between Fury and Straight Arrow. A cache of original rings was located in New York and many had lenses already in place. Gary located the wire loops to secure the slide in place. Interestingly the circular slide could be clipped with a hand-held paper hole punch. The ring was available for $12.95 plus the official coupon from *POW-WOW*. For non-members, this meant they would need to join *Pow-Wow* at $5.00, which would entitle them to the first five issues of *Pow-Wow* and the coupon, making the total price $17.95. The money and snapshot were sent to Gary Fugate, who made the slide and assembled the final product.

## 9. Gold Colored Plastic Rite-A-Lite Arrowhead and Radiant Message Pass Card (1951)

The Rite-A-Lite not only could write a message on the special "radiant" card, but could be used as a flashlight. There is a ¾" tubular center to house the assembly consisting of a small flashlight bulb, a spring, a battery and a plunger that has a small hole with which to attach a rawhide string or chain. The plunger has the Indian word "Ta-wato-ko" wrapped around the top and according to the assembly instructions it means; "light in night." The arrowhead has knapped

flares on both sides giving it a wedge look. The flares measure ½" at the arrow tip and extend to 2" at the other end. The words "Straight Arrow" are etched on both sides of the tubular center with an arrow motif and an Indian face molded between "straight" and "arrow" similar to other premiums. The entire arrow measures approximately 4¾" from the tip of the exposed light bulb to the plunger. The 4" x 2½" white "radiant" message card has a non-toxic florescent covering with a "pass card", a membership card to the Straight Arrow tribe, printed in black on white on the other side. *Pow-Wow* (Vol 5, No. 19 Fall 1990) offered a reproduction of the "pass card" printed in two colors (red and blue) on gold (yellow) card stock. The Rite-A-Lite Arrowhead was available for one Nabisco Shredded Wheat box top and 25¢. ME *Straight Arrow* #11, March 1951, advertised the premium on the last page of the comic. The script for January 30, 1951 (#251) mentions a "golden arrow" but it was not identified in the script as the Rite-A-Lite.

**10. Injun-Uity Book (1951)**

The last premium offered by Nabisco was the collection in a bound booklet of all 72 cards of Injun-uities Series 1 and 2, available for one Nabisco Shredded Wheat box top and 15¢. The Indian crafts book had a two color cover (red and blue). Located in Sheldon Stark's papers was a story of Steve Adams coming to the realization of being Straight Arrow which was never published; however, it was condensed and printed on the inside back cover of the Injun-Uity Book (both versions were reprinted in the Pow-Wow newsletter). The book was advertised on the back cover of ME *Straight Arrow* #19 (November 1951), and in the body of *Straight Arrow* #20 (December 1951), as well as in DC *Comic Cavalcade* #48 (Dec/Jan 1950/1951). *Boy's Life* magazine, the official publication of the Boy Scouts of America, for October 1951, had an ad for the Injun-Uity Book.

**11. The Straight Arrow "Injun-uity Wall Chart" (1951)**

This was a special offer of a wall chart available only to the Boy Scouts of America through *Boy's Life* magazine (official publication of the Boy Scouts). Advertisements for the wall chart appeared in the April and May 1951 editions of *Boy's Life* magazine. The 21" x 27" chart was free for collecting 12 Straight Arrow cards. The coupon required only that the "unit leader" fill it out with his signature, address and unit name or number attesting to the fact that he had received 12 Injun-uity cards (the collected cards were not to be sent to Nabisco), and the chart would be sent to the unit The wall chart reproduced 12 Injun-uities in blue on white stock with red used for the arrow across the top, lines dividing the card reproductions and "Nabisco Shredded Wheat" across the bottom and on the Nabisco symbol in the Shredded Wheat box depicted at the bottom.

**TV PUPPET THEATRE**

In 1952 Nabisco Shredded Wheat introduced a TV Puppet Theatre, a new series of cardboard dividers. The first of two sets included a double card with the finger puppets, full-color illustrations printed on white, of Straight Arrow, Packy, Steve Adams, Fury and villain Cactus Harry and announcer Eddy West as well as props of two feathers to paste on back of Straight Arrow's head, Straight Arrow with bow and arrow, Straight Arrow astride Fury and Straight Arrow's hand. Each item was die-cut for ease in removing the individual items for trimming. The remaining two inserts were printed in green ink on regular gray cardboard stock and could be either the instructions for the puppet theatre with opening and closing commercials or one of two play scripts: The Stage Raider or It's Mine, All Mine. The finger puppets had a slotted band to allow for various finger sizes when connected to form a circle for sliding over fingers. The shredded wheat box's back were marked to be cut out and form a TV set where the plays could be staged by following the action scripted on the cards. Children were advised not to remove the bottom flaps, cut out the TV screen section and secure the box to the "back" edge of a table. It was advised that they reinforce the finger puppet's band with cellophane tape after fitting it to the finger. The second finger puppet set was titled Big Fun Filled Show and was not Straight Arrow related.

## MERCHANDISE ITEMS

Advertisers' Service Division (ASD) or "Specialty Advertising, which ever name they were using at the moment," recalled John Walworth, vice president and art director, presented premium ideas to Nabisco for Straight Arrow. Walworth does not remember any idea being turned down. Walworth was creator/designer for the red feathered head band, signal drums, bandanna and slide, tribal patch and the mystic wrist kit. In an effort to cash in on the promotion investment by Nabisco on Straight Arrow, ASD was formed to secure licensing rights through Nabisco's Straight Arrow Enterprises to produce Straight Arrow merchandise items. ASD in turn created a catalogue to send to prospective buyers, F. W. Woolworth's, McClellan, W.T. Grant, S. H. Kress, SS Kresge (later Kmart), McCrory, G.C. Murphy and other "Five and Dime" outlets. Mutual radio outlets were encouraged to buy radio spots on or after the Straight Arrow radio show to promote Straight Arrow merchandise. The Advertisers' Service Division, Inc., which had an office and factory located on East 25th Street in New York, New York, sent out a colorful catalogue, an 11" x 17" flyer folded twice. The cover fold told the Straight Arrow story and the back had ordering information. The first open fold was a page with every item shown in full color. Completely opened the flyer listed all 10 items with pertinent information:

1. The Straight Arrow Lollypop Signal Drum was exactly as the Signal Drum Walworth created for Nabisco except that 12 cello-wrapped pops, for easy display, were inserted in the corrugated bottom. A rubber head and a knocker were attached as well as a multi-colored wrist cord. The drum sold retail for 39¢.

2. The Straight Arrow Comanche Chief War Drum was a larger version of the signal drum with a knocker, and came with an Indian headband with elastic strap and a multi colored neck cord attached. This 12" high drum retailed at 59¢.

3. The Straight Arrow Bandanna and Gold Plated Slide was an exact reproduction of the Nabisco premium designed by Walworth. The slide was described as also serving as a ring. The bandanna and slide retailed at 29¢.

4. The Straight Arrow Lollypop Headband was boxed with a cellophane window revealing the 8 cello-wrapped pops with two dyed turkey feathers and a headband with elastic and barbs attached. It retailed at 19¢ each.

5. Straight Arrow Jig Saw Puzzles were 12 different four-color illustrated puzzles on extra heavy fiber board, with 63 pieces, individually packed in a window envelope with an Indian motif printed on the outside and words "Straight Arrow" across the top. The puzzle illustrations were drawn by Fred L. Meagher and would appear on a variety of other ASD items. The puzzles retailed at 10¢ each.

6. The Straight Arrow Boxed Jig Saw Puzzle Assortment of 10 puzzles fitting the description of the individual assorted puzzle (#5 above). The collection came packed together in a windowed box. The 10 puzzles retailed at $1.00 per package.

7. Straight Arrow Framed Pictures were 12 assorted four-color action prints measured at 7" x 9" (the same illustrations as the 12 puzzles listed in #5 above), covered with a thin plastic sheet and mounted in a simulated birch bark frame without hanging hardware. The framed pictures retailed at 39¢ each.

8. Straight Arrow Coloring Book was a 48 page book with a four color cover, of illustrated Straight Arrow scenes, many done by Fred. L. Meagher. The book was printed on a 32 lb. novel newsprint, a high bulk newsprint with the superior finish most preferred by teachers and students, measuring 11" x 14" and retailing at 15¢. The coloring books were produce in Sandusky, Ohio. Later the manufacturers of the coloring book, Stephens Publishing Company of Sandusky, Ohio, would issue a 16 page Straight Arrow coloring book with a four-color cover with illustrations from ASD's version mostly drawn by Fred L. Meagher. The copyright reads by "Nabisco 1949." The paper is newsprint, but lighter weight than the original, and no retail price was attached. (Note: The book in Pow-Wow's collection appears to have never been circulated; in fact, it was later learned that someone had hundreds of copies for sale that came from a warehouse find. One could surmise that perhaps copyright or other infringements caused the book to never circulate.)

9. The Straight Arrow Latex Mask was a colorful Indian mask with elastic and barb attached. It came in assorted large and small sizes and retailed at 59¢ each.

10. The Straight Arrow Buffalo Horn was a plastic reproduction of a genuine horn with a built in buffalo call. A decal with Straight Arrow's name and an illustrated depiction of a Straight Arrow profile decorated the horn. A multi-colored cord for carrying was attached. The horn retailed at 39¢.

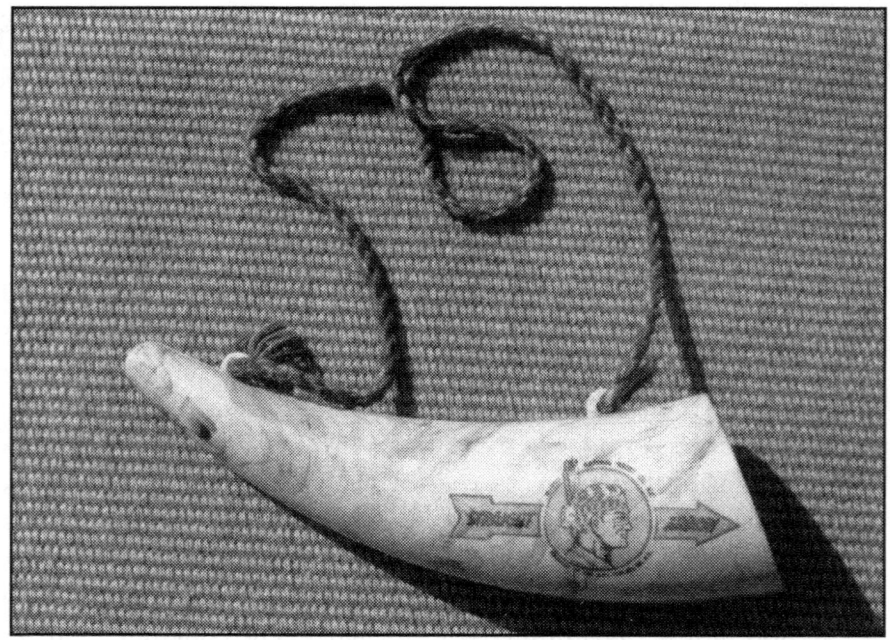

## JOHN C. WALWORTH

"How did I get involved with Straight Arrow?" Walworth reminisced. John C. Walworth's journey to "cardboard engineering" and to be Straight Arrow merchandise/premium creator had its beginning September 7, 1913, in New Rochelle, New York. As a child Walworth would copy figures from the funny paper. "I guess in the back of my mind I wanted to be a cartoonist!" He was editor of his high school yearbook in 1931 and "loaded it with cartoons in every style, mostly my own." Working a variety of jobs after graduation he decided to go to California. There in 1936 he started a career in animation working for Columbia, Universal and MGM. The critical and financial fury associated with Disney's *Snow White* sent him packing back to New York to work with Max Fleischer Studio on *Gulliver's Travels*, a major animated adventure to rival Disney and cash in on the success of *Snow White*. Walworth received an offer from Joe Oriolo, Felix the Cat artist, to replace a designer found Walworth switching from animation to creating advertising premiums, "It was quite a switch, but I decided to do it. The first cardboard design I did was a train for the cardboard dividers in the old Shredded Wheat boxes."

It was at this time he encountered Straight Arrow. Walworth would toss out ideas to Nabisco as possible premiums. "I don't recall they (Nabisco) ever rejected any of them." Walworth was vice president and art director of ASD, producers of various Straight Arrow items, which were manufactured by outside contractors, all under ASD's orders and supervision. Contracting with Nabisco's Straight Arrow Enterprises

Walworth and his partner, Bob Weil, created an impressive list of Straight Arrow premiums and merchandise items. The sudden shift of Nabisco advertisement dollars from radio to television ended the Straight Arrow radio program. Walworth lamented, "They dropped dead on us!"

Walworth continued in the child-appeal premium business, mostly with Gold Premium Company, where he designed promotions for various clients, one being Cracker Jack, for whom he created at least 600 items. In 1989, Walworth was honored with a exhibition of his creations at the University of Delaware entitled A Surprise Inside! The Work and Wizardry of John Walworth. Walworth died December 31, 1991.

## NOVEL NOVELTIES, INC

ME Straight Arrow #3 (June/July) advertised two target games that could be found in local stores or ordered from Novel Novelties of New York, New York:

1. The target practice game had a tin board with a circular target with circles of varying points and smaller circles across the top and at both corners. The weapon, a bow with a hand grip with a hole to allow the arrow to pass through, thus giving more aiming control. The "arrows" had suction cups on the ends.

2. The other was a tin board with various "outlaws" with varying point value for scoring. The "weapon" was a very simple bow device made of a dowel and a grip. The "bullet" was a small magnet with a feather attached. The string was drawn back "arrow" was positioned so that the "feathered magnet arrow" was launched toward the target. Both target games could be ordered for $1.00 each.

## STRAIGHT ARROW BOARD GAME

In 1950 Selchow and Righter introduced a Straight Arrow game into its already famous line-up of popular board games. The simple game was created by a private individual and remained in the Selchow and Righter Company catalog until 1956. The game consisted of a board with horseshoe directional paths with "perils" of Rustlers' Raids or Indian Attacks. There were four corner sites titled: Indian Camp, Broken Bow Ranch, Cave of Straight Arrow and Rustlers' Hideout. There were 15 metal steers, 4 wooden playing pawns (which looked like genie bottles), 18 golden arrow cards (printed in gold on red 1" x

1½" cards), one lariat wheel spinner and one metal Straight Arrow pawn (an Indian on horseback with a rifle, painted brown). The game consisted of roping steers and earning golden arrows. The winner would be the player with the highest score, based on steers (1 point each) and golden arrows (2 points each). A player could become Straight Arrow by landing in the Cave, thus replacing his pawn with the Straight Ar-

Alexander, Teresa and Bill look on as Blue celebrates winning the Straight Arrow Game.

row pawn. The player who becomes Straight Arrow rides on the trail of justice, and once justice has been served, either by Straight Arrow or a pawn, Straight Arrow returns to the cave. The cover drawn by Fred L. Meagher has Straight Arrow on Fury.

**OTHERS**

*The Playthings Directory* magazine dated 1951 advertised a Straight Arrow reversible Indian and cowboy outfit from Collegeville Flag & Mfg. Co. of Collegeville, Pennsylvania, with Philadelphia, Pennsylvania, and New York, New York addresses. It was touted as "Another Collegeville Exclusive from the popular western character of the National Biscuit Co. - radio program." The ad included a stylized drawing of Straight Arrow and the copyright symbol next to name "National Biscuit Co."

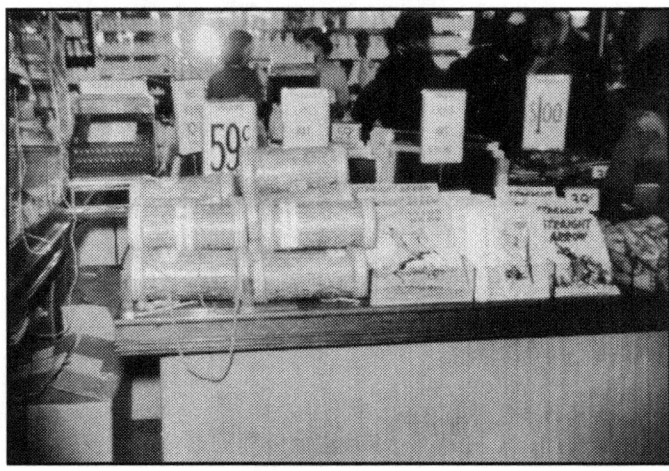

The Bell Syndicate promotional flyer listed items that were being "sold throughout the country" and available at wholesale prices for promotional use. Two of the items listed have yet to be verified as having been produced: a Straight Arrow Quiver Set and a Straight Arrow Mystery Picture Painting Set.

# Print Media

Perhaps the greatest impact on the remembrance of the Straight Arrow promotion of the late 40s and early 50s may have been due more to the print media than the radio broadcast. When the radio show moved from regional to nationwide broadcasting the Straight Arrow promotion went into motion. Nabisco introduced the Straight Arrow Injun-Uities Book One (a set of 36 numbered cards) into its Shredded Wheat cereal boxes as dividers between the biscuits. In 1949 a contract was worked out for the rights to publish the exploits of radio's Straight Arrow in a four-color comic book, and in 1950 Bell Syndicate began producing a daily Straight Arrow strip that had an initial market of 50 newspapers.

## INJUN-UITY

Nabisco issued the first set, Book One, of the Straight Arrow Injun-Uities into Shredded Wheat in 1949. These 4 x 7 inch gray cardboard cards were printed in blue ink for Book One (1949) and Two (1950), and in green ink for Books Three (1951) and Four (1952), a "book" being a full set of 36 cards. Each 36-card set had a cover card and table of contents card, and the cards were numbered consecutively beginning with the cover. There were a total of 144 different cards (however card 19, Poisonous Snakes, of Book One was replaced by Announcement for Book Two card, which was a totally different card making the actual total 145). Three different cards randomly inserted separated the four rows of three Shredded Wheat biscuits per box.

Fred L. Meagher (pronounced Marr), illustrator all four books, was listed as "Indian illustrator and authority." These cards were produced by the millions and are still readily available today. In 1951 the material in Books One and Two was collected together and produced as a stapled booklet, offered as a premium for 15¢ and one Nabisco Shredded Wheat book top. Also in

1951, an ad in *Boys Life* (official publication of the Boys Scout of America) offered a free "Injun-uity Wall Chart" measuring 21"x 27". The cards were advertised as "Indian Skills and Crafts Illustrated with 'how-to-do-it' pictures" which concisely describes the material offered on the Injun-Uity cards.

There is evidences that the Injun-Uity cards were cleverly promoted in the Straight Arrow radio show NABISCO commercials. "Mesquite Molly's really headed for trouble." reads a May 25, 1950 commercial. "Too bad she doesn't have Straight Arrow's Injun-Uity card number 23 (from Book One), which tells how to signal for help!" The commercial continues expounding the goodness of NABSICO Shredded Wheat and then adds how three cards were included in each package.

## STRAIGTH ARROW COMICS

After a decade of comic book experience Vincent (Vin) Sullivan finally stepped out on his own in 1943 to form Magazine Enterprises (ME). Sullivan's debut in the world of comics was as a co-editor of the newly formed National Allied Publication, which later merged into National Periodical, at which time Sullivan was named a full editor. One of the comics that Sullivan edited was *Action Comics* #1 (1938) where "Superman" made his first appearance marking the advent of modern comics. In 1940 he joined several others to form Columbia Comic Corporation and later formed ME. Entering comics in the 30's Sullivan was learning an industry that had no precedents or job descriptions. His dream was to issue comic books with all new material and not simply reprints of funny paper strips. With the formation of ME he was in the position to carry out this dream. In the beginning there were issues of reprints, but most comics published by ME consisted of new material. ME was just a small office in New York with a limited staff that included Raymond Krank as editor. Most of the writers and illustrators were professionals Sullivan had worked with in the past. The writers would turn in story scripts to the office and according to Fred Guardineer, who worked with Sullivan at National and Columbia, illustrators would pick up their checks and new assignments when they dropped off finished work. "We were all professional and Vin treated us as professionals. I do not recall any work being returned for rework."

In 1949 Sullivan worked out a deal with Nabisco's bureau "Straight Arrow Enterprises" for the publishing rights to depict radio Straight Arrow's exploits in a four-color comic book format. Gardner Fox was given the title for scripting and is credited with writing every script (Sullivan in a letter dated November 14, 1984, disputes this by writing, "of the several writers connected with the book, the only one who comes to mind is Gardner Fox.") Fox produced 8,000 pages for ME. Fred L. Meagher, already familiar with the character of Straight Arrow with work for Nabisco, was recommended as the illustrator. According to Bill Black's *Best of the West* (*Golden-Age Greats* Vol. 7) Frank Frazetta was also under consideration for the assignment. However Meagher was given the job and went on to draw every ME Straight Arrow story in *Straight Arrow* comics (1-55) and *Best of the West* (1-11) stories as well as all the art chores of the one-shot *Fury* (Straight Arrow's horse) comic. He also did all the covers on the ME *Straight Arrow* comics, except issue #3 and #22, which were drawn by Frank Frazetta. *Straight Arrow* #1 appeared with a dateline of February/March 1950 with a banner across the top of the magazine that read, "See your favorite radio character!!!!" According to Sullivan all the materials prepared for Straight Arrow were required to go to Nabisco's legal department before publication. Sullivan wrote in a letter (March 23, 1984) that "Straight Arrow was not the cornerstone of ME—however, it did become the periodical with its (ME's) largest circulation." Bell Syndicate's promotional material for the comic strip indicated *Straight Arrow* #2 sold out at 600,000 copies and issue #3 and #4 would have a print run "of almost a million each…sellouts expected!"

## VINCENT SULLIVAN

Vin Sullivan's introduction to the comics was from an early love for the Sunday funnies. He was always drawing cartoons and considered cartooning as a career. The New York Daily News bought several of his sport cartoons, which led him, at a rather young age, to apply for the newspaper's position of sport cartoonist when there was an opening. He was not hired. "I think I might have been too young" is how Sullivan figured it years later. However, he was always on the look out for cartooning openings. Sullivan did not remember how he learned that Major Malcolm Wheeler-Nicholson was forming a comic book publishing organization, but soon after the first meeting, he was thrust into a new venture and comic history as a co-editor of National Allied Publications.

Sullivan was born in Brooklyn, New York, on June 5, 1911 and at the age of 24 joined Nicholson. Because there were no job descriptions for editors of comic books Sullivan was forced to learn all aspects of comic publishing with "on the job training." In 1938 Nicholson, who was deeply in debt to his distributor, found his company reformed into National Periodical, and Sullivan was advanced to full editor. Sullivan found himself thrust into comic history with his editorship on *Action* #1 which debuted Superman, certainly the most important comic book series ever published. Later Sullivan would encourage Bob Kane to create a costumed character, thus resulting in the debut of Batman in *Detective Comics* #27 (1939).

A year later, Sullivan joined with two others to form Columbia Comic Corporation. Many writers and illustrators from the National days submitted work to Columbia. Sullivan's hope with Columbia was to have original comic stories as the foundation of the firm. He thought they were "dragging their heels" as he put it and decided to launch out on his own. In 1943 Magazine Enterprises (ME) was formed (in the early years the publishing firm would fall under a variety of names, Life's Romance Publishing Company-Chicago, Compix, Inc. – New York). Under the editorship of Raymond Krank and the acquired expertise of Sullivan, ME would publish one of the most diverse and lively line-ups of comic books. Tapping the western silver screen popularity Sullivan began signing a variety of cowboy stars. His approach to marketing was to have a trial period for a feature in ME's *A-1* line-up and if the sales warranted it the book might get its own title. He published war books, jungle books, horror, humor, teen books etc.; interestingly Sullivan never published a "super hero" book at ME. ME was discontinued in 1958 after ME experienced a loss of revenue. Sullivan blamed the poor comic market on the advent of television. Sullivan never returned to the comic business. He did secure the rights to market a "Popeye" peanut butter product, but the competitive market caused this to fail. In 1993, Sullivan expressed the possibility of bringing some of the ME characters to television as animated features, but this was never brought to fruition. During the early 90's he begin to receive belatedly the recognition he deserved for his role in comic history. He was guest and panelist at the San Diego Comic Convention in 1998. Vin Sullivan died February 3, 1999.

## GARDNER F. FOX

Gardner Francis Fox was a most unlikely candidate to be a comic book author. Fox, a childhood friend of Vin Sullivan, was schooled as a lawyer. A graduate of St. John's University School of Law, Fox was encouraged by Sullivan to write comic scripts for National. As Fox continued to pursue his law career, he wrote pulp magazine stories and comic scripts until finally giving up law altogether to become a notable and popular author. Born in Brooklyn, New York in May 20, 1911, the same year as Sullivan, Fox followed his friend Sullivan from National to Columbia and on to ME, becoming one of the most prolific comic writer of the Golden Age of comics. He was the primary scripter at ME. After ME, Fox went on to become a major figure and innovator in the Silver Age of comics. While at ME, Fox is credited with writing all the stories of Straight Arrow and under various aliases, Russ and/or Ray Gardner, wrote all the scripts for Bell Syndicate's Straight Arrow daily strips. Gar, as Fox signed his letters, passed away in New Jersey on December 24, 1986.

## FRED L MEAGHER

When Fred L. Meagher became associated with Nabisco's Straight Arrow promotion in 1949, he had already been involved with many popular culture icons. In 1936 his illustrations appeared on Hershey Publications' short-lived pulps, *Dan Dunn Detective Magazine* and *Tailspin Tommy Air Adventures*. From 1935 through World War II his illustrations appeared in various aviation publications and books produced and written by Assen Jordonanoff. In 1937 his now distinctive drawing style appeared on *Gulf Funny Weekly* "Wings Winfare." This Gulf Oil Company giveaway had a weekly print run of 3 million at its peak. In 1941 his work was in *Tom Mix Comics* (a Ralston-Purina four color comic giveaway later titled *Tom Mix Commandos*) in various stories as well as the Tom Mix features.

When Vin Sullivan, publisher and owner of Magazine Enterprises comics, obtained the publishing rights to do Straight Arrow in a four-color format Fred L. Meagher was selected as artist. It is interesting to note that the early ME *A-1* stories were strips reprinted from the Chicago Tribune where Meagher introduced "Vista," a story of a plucky girl and her horse which appeared on August 30, 1942 in the *Chicago Tribune Comic Book Magazine*. At Magazine Enterprises he not only did all the Straight Arrow stories, but he also took on the illustrative chores of "Dan Brand and Tipi" a back-up feature in *The Durango Kid* (later to be collected together as *White Indian*). While at ME, he was also drawing the *Broncho Bill* comic strip for United

Features Syndicate, which evolved into *Buffalo Bill* on February 17, 1955. (It is interesting to note that Meagher's wife Ruthanne, part Indian, was the model for Bluebird in the *Buffalo Bill* strip as well as Blue Cloud in the *Straight Arrow* comics). The dates for the *Broncho Bill/Buffalo Bill* strips have not been confirmed, but records show Meagher was drawing the strip in 1953 and continued until it discontinued in 1956. The demise of ME and *Buffalo Bill* marked the end of Meagher's comic work.

Frederick Lawrence Meagher was born in Clearfield, Pennsylvania, on April 11, 1912. Ted, as he was called, began to show a flair for the arts at an early age. At 16 he enrolled in the International Corresponding Schools in art (an outstanding alumnus honor was bestowed on Meagher by ICS in the 50s). In 1932 Ted entered Alfred University, the oldest co-educational college in New York and, at the time, considered the foremost college in commercial ceramics.

Meagher illustrated Straight Arrow merchandise items created and produced by Advertisers' Service Division (ASD) under the art direction of John Walworth. ASD created many of the premiums for Nabisco Shredded Wheat as well as a full array of merchandise items, such as puzzles, coloring books, framed pictures, etc. The rearing Fury with Straight Arrow was depicted on the Selchow and Righter Straight Arrow board game which was manufactured from 1951until 1956. To meet deadlines Meagher taught Ruthanne the art of inking and lettering; thus the long days were eased and the deadlines met.

With the end of his comic career Meagher moved again into industrial design by joining American Can, makers of Dixie Cup brand items. The Meagher style that thrilled comic readers would occasionally appear on Dixie Cup promotions. One such promotion, "Round-Up Design," depicted cutout figures of Indians and cowboys reminiscent of the Straight Arrow puppet cutouts in Nabisco Shredded Wheat in 1953.

Throughout his life Meagher enjoyed drawing huge paintings depicting scene from the old west. Craig Flessel, who freelanced work for Magazine Enterprises, remembered Meagher, "He wanted to be a western artist. He wore a cowboy outfit and had a few horses on Long Island." While living in New Jersey in the mid 50's Meagher bought land near Blairstown, naming it Circle M Ranch. When he moved west he bought a ranch in the true tradition of the west, naming it Circle M as well.

Linnea Andersson-Wintle remembered Fred L. Meagher in New Jersey and wrote; "We lived on Swede Mine Road, just up from the Meagher family in the early 50s, walking distance outside Dover, NJ - when it was rural and sparsely populated. The hill we lived on had only a few houses then, remnants of old iron ore mines, and a mica mine. I remember Mr. Meagher proudly riding his stallion up to my house. I think he lived as he drew. As a little girl, I remember thinking he was a cowboy. I remember the comic dividers in Shredded Wheat, but usually only caught a glimpse of them as they passed into my two older brothers' hands for keeping. I have a Christmas card that was sent to my family in 1953 from the Meagher family."

Meagher died January 26, 1976, in Smith Valley, Nevada. He was able to enjoy three years on a western ranch amid all the scenery he depicted in Straight Arrow. Fred. L. Meagher, who always articulated his last name as "Marr" insisting on this Celtic version over the usual accepted "Mee-ger," is remembered today because his illustrative work was seen by millions through the various product promotions and because his name appeared on most of his illustrative work, something not commonly done during the Golden Age of comics. However he never got fandom recognition.

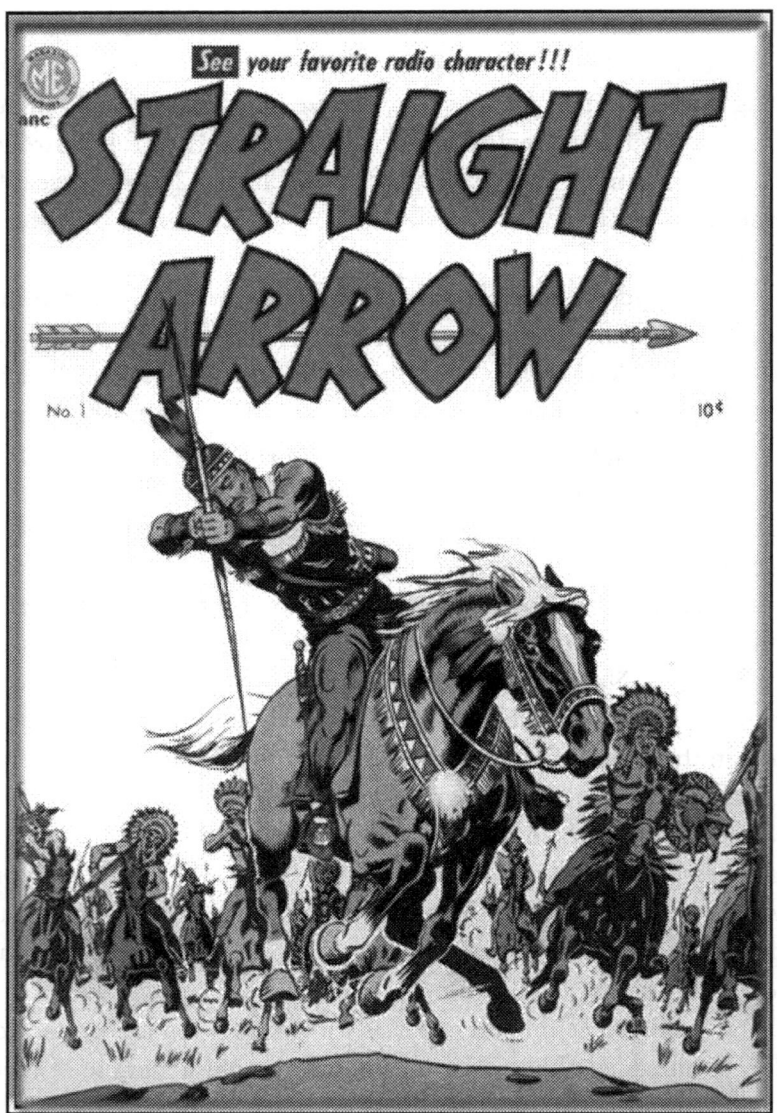

## STRAIGHT ARROW IN THE COMICS

STRAIGHT ARROW was introduced to comic readers with a dateline of February/March 1950 and ended with issue #55 dated March 1956. Vin Sullivan, publisher and editor of Magazine Enterprises (ME), made arrangement with Nabisco's bureau "Straight Arrow Enterprises" to depict the adventures of Straight Arrow in comic book format. The *Straight Arrow* comic was issued every other month until issue #4, when it began a monthly schedule. The monthly schedule reverted to semi-monthly with April/May (1952) #24, returning to monthly with issue #40 (December 1954) and remaining monthly until cancellation in 1956. Fred L. Meagher drew every Straight Arrow story and every cover, except issue #3 and #22, which were drawn by Frank Frazetta. Meagher drew all the Straight Arrow appearances in ME's *Best of the West* and ME's reprints *Great Westerns*. Gardner L. Fox has been given credit for writing if not all the stories most of them. Sullivan said it became his best selling book. The books were all copyrighted by Nabisco, except the last issue where the indicia display had ME as copyrighter, but Sullivan said that was a mistake and the book was still under copyright to Nabisco. There were reprints as well as foreign editions of *Straight Arrow*. The American reprints were in the 1960s. Skwald reprinted the story The Dynamiters (from *Straight Arrow* #6, October 1950) in *Bravados* (No. 1), 1971 under the character name of Swift Arrow. There were foreign reprints issued especially in the United Kingdom as *Straight Arrow* and Brazil as *Flecha Ligeira* Magazine (1955).

There were several recurring players in the comic series. Though opposites in virtues, Black Feather matched Straight Arrow in skill and his horse Diablo rivaled Fury. Nan Fellows and Fawn were two "love" interests that not only appeared in the Straight Arrow comic book but also made appearances in the short-lived newspaper strip, as did Straight Arrow's young friend Tioga. Blue Cloud and Pedro Bombo also appeared on several occasions.

In the early issues there were one and two page fillers, some illustrated stories others narrative stories. Only those stories that might interest collectorsare included in the descriptions of each book.

(Red Hawk was the 3rd story unless indicated otherwise)

## 1950

Across the top of the front cover ran a banner that read, "See your favorite radio character!!!" The first issue introduced Straight Arrow using the same opening signature as the radio show. The language and basic structure of these early stories imitated Sheldon Stark's radio scripts. The second story had the same title as the nationwide premiere radio show #40, February 7, 1949, and with characters of the same name. Two stories depicted the use of a small golden arrow (similar to the poorly received premium of the Golden Arrow Tie Clasp or barrette for girls issued in 1949). The inside front and back cover reproduced Injun-Uity Cards

#1    1. Straight Arrow
1 page filler, Lodgepole Lore illustrated by Bob Powell
2. Roaring River
3. Tales of the Tipi (Not a Straight Arrow story or a Red Hawk story, illustrated by Bob Powell)
4. Apache Vengeance

The second story, in this issue, has the same title and characters as radio show #60, March 24, 1949. There are some differences, but minute. A Nabisco ad appears on the back cover for the Injun-Uity cards (Book One) as well as reproductions of Injun-Uities cards on the inside front and back cover.

#2    1. The Peril of the Pioneers!
2. Land of our Fathers!
3. The Men of the Green Feathers
4. The Death Moccasin!

The banner across the top of this issue read, "Hear Straight Arrow Coast to Coast on the Mutual Network (with a Mutual logo)." This issue reproduced portions of a Injun-Uities in color as well as ads for two Straight Arrow target games sold through Novel Novelties, Inc. On the inside front was a reproduction of an Injun-Uities card, on the back inside cover was a coupon encouraging readers to express their interest in having the Straight Arrow newspaper in their local paper. A Nabisco ad for the Mystic Wrist Kit appeared on the back cover.

#3    1. The Killer Bear!
2. The Doctor of Medicine Hat!
3. In the Earthshaker
4. The Traps of Terror!

Nabisco's ad for the Injun-Uities cards on the back cover. A reproduction of an Injun-Uities card was on the inside front cover and on the inside of the back cover was the announcement that the book was now being published monthly as well as a coupon soliciting readers interest in having the newspaper strip published in their local newspapers.

#4    1. The Battle of the Giants!
2. The Man who held the Lightning!
3. The All-Seeing Eye!
4. The Buffalo Hide of Peace!

On the back cover was a Nabisco ad for the Straight Arrow (gold-colored) Arrow Clip "An exact copy of the golden arrow that Straight Arrow leaves wherever he goes!" This is the infamous tie clip or girl's barrette. A reproduction of an Injun-Uities card was on the inside front cover and on the inside of the back cover was the notice that the book was being published monthly as well as a coupon soliciting readers interest in having the newspaper strip published in their local newspapers.

#5
1. The Ghost of Straight Arrow!
2. Mission of Hate!
3. Quest of the Rain Drum!
4. Straight Arrow's Great Leap...!

This issue announced the return of the Straight Arrow to the Mutual Broadcasting System, Tuesday, September 12. The show took a summer hiatus with June 22, 1950 (#210) and returned September 12 with four repeat shows. A Nabisco Shredded Wheat ad was on the back cover.

#6
1. Lances of the Cheyenne!
2. The Dynamiters! Skwald *Bravados* (No. 1) reprinted this story in 1971, under the character name of "Swift Arrow".
3. The Bow that would not Bend!
4. The Boy from Back East!

The Straight Arrow Tribal Patch was advertised on the last page of the comic book. On the back inside cover was a 1 page story (ad), Know Your Airlines, illustrated by Bob Powell.

#7
1. Comanche Country!
2. The Sand Ship!
3. The Man Who Shot the Moon!
4. The Death Warning!

An ad for the new series of the Injun-Uities manual – Book II was advertised on the inside front cover.

#8
1. The Flaming Trail!
2. Robbery Rides the Rails!
3. Cheyenne Challenge
   1 page filler, The Rhyming Robber!, illustrated by Dick Ayers
4. Fang - Hound of Terror

## 1951

The Gold Nugget Picture Ring was advertised on the back cover with Injun-Uities on the inside front and back cover.

#9
1. The Claim Jumpers!
2. The Trial of Flying Cloud!
3. The Magic Plant!
4. Apache Terror!

The new series of Straight Arrow Injun-Uity manual, Book II was advertised on the back cover.

#10
1. The River from Nowhere!
2. Terror's Army Rides the Plaines!
3. The Man Who Rode the Moonlight!
4. The Noose!

The Rite-A-Lite Arrowhead and Radiant Message Pass Card premium was advertised on last page of the comic book.

#11
1. The Valley of Time
2. The Salt War
3. The Giant in the Mist
4. Ghost Gang

Nabisco Shredded Wheat ad appeared on the last page of the comic book.

#12
1. The Return of Black Feather!
2. RED HAWK – The Killers on the Cliffs!
3. The Treasure Coach!
4. The Pipe of ~~Peace~~ War!

Book II of the Straight Arrow Injun-Uity manual was advertised on the inside front cover.

#13
1. The Conquistadors Return
2. Treachery's Banner
3. The Dead Man's Trail!
4. The Revenge of the Mountain Spirit

This issue bannered across the front cover, "The Original Indian Hero of Radio Fame." The last page of the comic had a Nabisco Shredded Wheat ad.

#14  1. The Bullet-Proof Badmen!
2. Fighting Peacemaker
3. The Devil Bag!
4. Buffalo Killers

In June, 1951, the season's last arrow show advertised *Straight Arrow* issue #15. A Nabisco Shredded Wheat ad, located in the body of the comic book, appeared with a message near the bottom for the reader to listen to Straight Arrow adventures on Mutual Broadcasting System

#15  1. The Disappearing Lake
2. Gunsmoke Trail!
3. The Coup-Stick of Crying-Calf!
4. The Young Chief

"The Original Indian Hero of Radio Fame" banner on the front cover appeared again and continued until Straight Arrow #25. A Nabisco Shredded Wheat ad printed in the body of the comic book did not mention the radio show.

#16  1. The Magic Medicine-Man!
2. Rustler's Convention!
3. The Testing of Red Wolf!
4. The Renegade's Oath!

Nabisco Shredded Wheat ad appeared on the inside of the front cover with no mention of the radio show.

#17  1. Apache Raiders
2. Trapped in Bat Cave!
3. The Canyon Killers!
4. Death by Inches

The Nabisco Shredded Wheat ad published in the body of the comic book did not mention the radio adventures of Straight Arrow.

#18  1. The Educated Outlaws
2. RED HAWK - The Fanged Killer!
3. Death from Nowhere!
4. The Ugly One

A Nabisco ad appeared for the Injun-Uity Manual, a collection of the first two series of Injun-Uities was printed on the back cover.

#19  1. War Cry of the Thunderbird
     2. The Desert Demon!
     3. The Happy Hunting Ground
     4. The Curse of the Fire God

A Nabisco ad appeared for the Injun-Uity Manual, a collection of the first two series of Injun-Uities was printed in the body of the comic.

#20  1. The Sky-Hook Gang!
     2. The Shield of Straight Arrow
     3. The Truth Tomahawk!
     4. The Snake Terror!

**1952**

#21  1. Bloody Bridge!
     2. RED HAWK – Death Trap!
     3. The Story of Fury
     4. A Friendly Foe! (Intro of Nan Fellows)

#22  1. Steve Adams, Badman!
     2. RED HAWK - Beast of the Bayous!
     3. The Luck of Loud Calf!
     4. Trail by Fury!

#23  1. The Peace-breakers
     2. Satan's Desperadoes
     3. The Battle of the Everglades!
     4. The Decision?

#24  1. The Dragons of Doom!
     2. The Brave who hated Straight Arrow
     3. The Beast of the Bloody Trail!
     4. The Vanishing Buffalo!

#25  1. The Deathless One!
     2. Straight Arrow's Magic!
     3. The Ghost of Hiawatha!
     4. The Swamp Rats!

#26  1. The Choosing of a Chief!
     2. RED HAWK – The Hungry Giant!
     3. Wanted The Killers of Echo Canyon!
     4. Death to Steve Adams! (story continues and concludes in issue #27

#27  1. Arrow of Justice!
     2. The Four Horseman of Hate!
     3. The Claws of Death!
     4. The Manhood of Takona

## 1953

#28  1. The Challenge of Pedro Bombo!
     2. The Man who hated Fury!
     3. The Winged Men!
     4. The Return of the Thunderer!

#29  1. The Laughing Crime!
     2. RED HAWK – Blood on Blackfoot Pass!
     3. The Thing in the Ice!
     4. Top Secret

#30  1. The Ghost Apaches!
     2. Straight Arrow's Secret!
     3. Black Arrow of Death!
     4. The Mysterious Stranger!

#31  1. The Treasure of Pedro Bomba(o)
     2. The Invisible Terror
     3. Satan's Sanctuary
     4. RED HAWK – The Flying Horror!

#32  1. The Man without a Face!
     2. Trial by Battle!
     3. The Vengeance of the Weasel!
     4. Bait for the Hangman's Noose!

#33  1. Kin of the Wild!
     2. Jailbreak at Fort Danger! (Page out of sequence)
     3. The Bear-Stick
     4. Straight Arrow: Badman?

**1954**

#34  1. Madman's Empire!
     2. The River Robbers!
        (3D effect developed by artist, Frank Bolle
        and editor, Ray Krank
     3. The Demon Bear
     4. Straight Arrow – Wild West Star!

The Straight Arrow TV Puppet Theatre, a cut out on the back of the shredded wheat box, which included full color Finger Puppet of Straight Arrow, Packy, Fury and two scripts inserted in the box were advertised by Nabisco on the insidse front cover. The panel violator promoted "Straight Arrow's adventures are now in 200 suburban newspapers in the New York area" in the last panels of the third story, The Savage Student.

#35  1. Outlaw Death-Warrant!
     2. RED HAWK – The Woman Warriors
     3. The Savage Student!
     4. Date With Death!

#36  Entire issue reprinted in Great Western #1
     1. Danger Trail!
     2. Terror in the Night!
     3. Lands beyond the Sunset
     4. Return from Death!

#37  1. A Birthday Present for Polly
     2. RED HAWK – The Shaman's Curse
     3. Warrior's Blanket
     4. The Secret of the Secret Cave!

#38  1. The Mystery of the Missing Herd
     2. The Saga of Bent Bow & Straight Arrow
     3. The Sands of Doom
     4. The Abominable Snowman

#39  1. The Vanishing Stagecoaches
     2. No title – (Title page closing "…rode the wild-haired shape of terror…")
     3. The Canyon Beast
     4. Showdown in Skeleton Canyon

#40  1. The Secret of the Spanish Specters
     2. The Executioners of Straight Arrow
     3. Two Guards for Death
     4. The Haunted Village

## 1955

A map depicting Straight Arrow's home range was printed in full color in this issue.

#41  1. The Siege at Broken Bow!
     2. Straight Arrow's Ride
     3. The Weapon Maker!
     4. The Man Who Chased Death!

#42  Entire issue reprinted in Heroes of the West – Gunfighters #10 (Super Comics)
     1. The Iron Horse of Indian Gulch
     2. The Grim Pursuit
     3. The Man Who Looked for Trouble
     4. RED HAWK – Men with Dog Faces!

Blaze, a dog, is introduced in this story and becomes a part of the Straight Arrow "team" and is depicted in several issues. This also marks the first appearance of the Comic Code symbol of Approval on the cover.

#43  1. Blaze
     2. The Robber from Beyond
     3. The City of Gold!
     4. The Last Arrow

#44  1. The Shield of Sleepy Wolf!
     2. Champion of Evil!
     3. Bad Medicine Man!!
     4. The Men who Frightened Straight Arrow!

#45  1. Straight Arrow Will Die!
     2. Sure Death in the Wild West
     3. Lorelei of the Snows
     4. The Marked Man

#46  1. The Man with the Scar
     2. The Fence Stealers
     3. The Rope Hand!
     4. Doom Stalks the Treasure Seeker

#47  1. The Menace of the Grey Wolves
     2. The Telltale Beads
     3. The Lost Medicine Bag
     4. Straight Arrow, Bandit

#48  Entire issue reprinted in Great Western #9 (I.W.)
     1. The Treasure of Don Carlos
     2. Tyrant of the Snows
     3. A Day for Straight Arrow
     4. RED HAWK – Renegade Trap

#49  1. Battle of the Giants
     2. The Train Robbers of Horseshoe Bend
     3. The Voice of Howling Dog!
     4. Two Hours to Doom

#50  1. Perilous Cargo
     2. RED HAWK – Capture at the Waterhole
     3. No title (in word balloon on splash page: "Look Out! It's Straight Arrow!")
     4. The Girl from the Desert

#51  1. The Mystery of the Frightened Boy!
     2. RED HAWK – Message for the Chief
     3. Goes East!
     4. Fangs of Justice

#52  1. The Rival Rascals
     2. The Spirit in the Bag
     3. The Disappearance of Bigfoot
     4. Doom of the North Wind

**1956**

#53  1. The Men who Bought Trains!
        (This story was reprinted in black and white from the original art and issued as an insert in Pow-Wow vol. 7 #29-30 1993)
     2. The Lost Wagons
     3. The Mark of the Wolf
     4. Vengeance Trail!

#54  Entire issue reprinted in Blazing Six Guns #18 (I.W. Super Comics)
     1. Captured by the Osages!
     2. Danger in the Cards!
     3. A Cargo of Doom!
     4. The Golden Peril!

This final issue depicts Straight Arrow on the cover in full chief regalia looking somewhat pensive and slightly forlorn.

#55  1. The Painted Man!
     2. The Second Childhood of Packy McCloud
     3. The Defeated Brave!
     4. The Gold Fever!

Great Western #9 (A1 #105)
Reprint Straight Arrow – lead story issue #1

Great Western #10 (A1 #113)
Reprint The Death Moccasin! – issue #2

Straight Arrow's Fury
1-4 All stories titled "Fury Straight Arrow's Golden Stallion"

Straight Arrow in "Best Of The West"
#1 Giant Killer
#2 The Face of the Devil
#3 The Curse of the Skulls
#4 The Marks of a Warrior
#5 The Man Who Killed Straight Arrow
#6 The Bow of Bear Claw
#7 The Big Frame-Up
#8 The Pits of Peril
#9 The Hunted
#10 The Law of the Arrow
#11 The Hunter and the Hunted
#12 No Straight Arrow story

Red Hawk #11
(There was only one issue of Red Hawk drawn by Bob Powell who drew the Red Hawk stories in *Straight Arrow* comics.)
1. Perilous Pet!
2. The Helpless Warrior!
3. The Death Dolls!
4. Tests for a Warrior!

## DAILY STRIP

As time marches on the information regarding the Straight Arrow comic strip becomes more blurred. Bell Syndicate acquired McClure Syndicate in the mid '50s and became Bell-McClure Syndicate. The current owners of Bell Syndicate, United Features Syndicate, which acquired Bell-McClure in 1972, have no records concerning the strip. The promotional page sent to newspapers had no dates listed. The strips reprinted in Pow-Wow, from *The State* newspaper headquartered in Columbia, South Carolina, had no date listed on the first 13 strips, but number 13 was dated July 3, 1950 and the last strip was August 4, 1951. This starting date agrees with ads in ME *Straight Arrow* #3, #4 and #5 dated June/July, August and September 1950 respectively, where readers were encouraged to fill out a coupon in the ad requesting the appearance of Straight Arrow in their daily paper. The completed coupons were to be sent to ME, not Bell Syndicate. The pull sheets of the strips in the Pow-Wow archives have the dates June 19, 1950, penned on the first set of strips. Beginning

One of the Sunday pages prepared by Certa and Belfi, but never published.

with strip 13 dates are printed on the pull sheet, the first being "Release Week of July 3, 1950" with the last reading "Release Week of July 30, 1951," which agrees with *The State* newspaper dates. These pull sheets from Bell Syndicate are rumored to have been from the estate of writer Fox. The last sheet has a cryptic message penciled at the bottom, "1 wk. get him out (Straight Arrow was depicted in a portable stock around his neck and his hands tied behind him) & finish up the best you can." Howard Culver in his remarks at an old time radio convention indicated that the canceling of the Straight Arrow radio show was made after the show went off the air for the summer. John Walworth, art direction of ASD, complained to Pow-Wow that the Straight Arrow promotion "dropped dead" on them.

In an ad from *New York World-Telegram* and *The Sun* dated August 28, 1950, Straight Arrow was introduced to the readership as just beginning in these two newspapers, which means that if every strip ran it would have gone into September, 1951. It is also noted that in *Straight Arrow* #35 (March/April 1954) a violator in the last two panels of the second story "The Savage Student" reads, "Straight Arrow's adventures are now in 200 suburban newspapers in the New York area."

Straight Arrow strip illustrators, John Belfi and Joe Certa, had worked together at Harvey Publications and on *The Durango Kid* at ME. The two agreed to take on the Straight Arrow comic strip when approached by Ray Krank of ME, even though, according to Belfi, both had an extremely heavy work schedule. They created 13 strips (a header and 12 dailies) from scripts by Gardner Fox (a.k.a. Ray Gardner and later Russ Gardner). Nabisco approved and Straight Arrow appeared in an initial list of 50 newspapers. Martin Demuth was the primary letterer. Several months after the strip had premiered the syndicate requested two Sunday pages, which were drawn but according to Belfi were never published because of a financial disagreement that could not be resolved. Belfi recalled that he and Certa worked directly with Nabisco, where all pencils with lettering went to Nabisco's legal department prior to completion. Belfi complained in a letter (dated 1982) about the Straight Arrow stories, "At the time, I thought the daily stories were terrible—one of the primary reasons Joe [Certa] and I decided to drop it." Belfi and Certa continued illustrating comics, not in tandem, in solo careers with various publishers.

## JOHN BELFI

John Belfi worked on approximately 500 comics, most unsigned. Today, everyone involved with comic production is given recognition, but not so when Belfi entered the comic field a half century ago.

"At about 12 [years old] I mailed some drawings to a local newspaper - and they were published!" Thus began the illustrator career for Belfi. But he had to wait until he was 14 years old to officially join the ranks of the professionals.

The Belfi family moved to the Bronx when John Belfi, who was born in Suffern, New York, August 3, 1924, was 14 years old. Here he learned that cartoonist Frank Frollo lived several blocks away. Belfi met Frollo and soon he was assisting him after school and on weekends in Frollo's studio. As an

apprentice, Belfi first cleaned up pages and later inked backgrounds. Later he was assigned features to ink and within six months he was doing full pages. At the time Frollo was doing *Buck Jones* for Dell and other western and adventure stories. Belfi attended New York School of Industrial Art while he continued freelancing. From 1938 until 1943 Belfi worked with many illustrators and a variety of publishers. In 1943 he joined the Army-Air Corps-Air Transportation Command stationed in the far east, returning to civilian life and comic book illustrating in 1946. In 1950, he joined with Joe Certa to draw *The Durango Kid* for Magazine Enterprises (ME). Belfi recalled, "Joe Certa and I worked together as a team for several years prior to producing the daily Straight Arrow strips for Bell Syndicate." Ray Krank, editor at ME, approached Belfi and Certa about adding the strip to their "extremely heavy" work load. The twosome created 12 strips from scripts by Gardner Fox (aka Russ/Ray Gardner) for Bell and Nabisco's approval. The strip had an immediate market of 50 newspapers. Each strip had to be mailed to Nabisco for approval by its legal department. Certa penciled and Belfi inked and Martin Demuth was the primary letterer. Several months later the team was asked to create 2 Sunday pages. The Sundays never were published, according to Belfi, "due to financial disagreements which could not be resolved." The daily strip lasted less than two years. Belfi continued in the comic field until 1955 when he "drifted" into advertising, eventually owing his own ad agencies. He taught at Joe Kubert School of Cartoon and Graphic Arts. Belfi died in Tobyhanna, Pennsylvania on October 2, 1995.

**JOE CERTA**

Joe Certa was born in Manhattan, New York, June 2, 1919, and attended public schools in the City. At school he began to show an interest in art and drawing. In high school, he visited various cartoonists with a school mate. Upon graduating Certa began working with Ham Fisher, one of the cartoonists he had visited, on the Joe Palooka strip, which he did from 1938 until 1942. Certa choose not to go to college, but instead opted to attend the Art Student League. In 1941, prior to joining the Army, Certa married Olympia. While in the service he was stationed at a communications center (Fort Lee, Petersburg, Virginia), where he produced brochures and promotional material and drew a strip about a soldier, "Will B. Wright." The strip appeared in both the Richmond Times Dispatch and the Philadelphia Inquirer. After his discharge, Certa freelanced for various comic publishing companies. He worked in tan-

Two Straight Arrow display stand-up poster promoting Nabisco Shredded Wheat and the local Mutual affiliate airing the radio show. Gary Fugate, collector, is pictured in photograph on the right.

dem with John Belfi and they teamed to do the Straight Arrow dailies. Certa moved to commercial work, primarily in the advertising and film-strip market, when the comic market experienced a downward trend in the late 50s. Certa's career spanned 50 years and included work that entertained and work intended to educate. He died February 15, 1986.

**MISCELLANEOUS**—Advertisement in other publications, store promotions, newspaper advertisement, bus advertisements

When the Straight Arrow radio show premiered nationwide February 7, 1949, Nabisco had already put into motion a well orchestrated promotion. *Sponsor* magazine, December 19, 1949, touted Straight Arrow as Nabisco's biggest investment. Nabisco worked closely with Mutual Broadcasting System by sending station managers merchandising kits which included posters, newspaper matted layouts, etc., all linked to promotions for Nabisco Shredded Wheat as well as for the local radio station carrying the program There were two stand-up posters both depicting Straight Arrow with his finger pointing at the customers and proclaiming in print "Listen to Straight Arrow...buy" with an directional arrow pointing to a box of Nabisco Shredded Wheat. Below the cereal box was a blank space available for the local radio station's call letters. One was drawn full size and the other only depicting the upper portion of Straight Arrow's body. Comic books were another source of advertising, not only in the ME *Straight Arrow* comic, but comics published by others, especially books with Indian heroes. There was a banner for buses and subways that advertised the Mutual line-up of "air-ventures": Bobby Benson, Straight Arrow, Tom Mix and Capt. Midnight. The daily strips were promoted in the Straight Arrow comics as well as in promotional flyers from Bell Syndicate. Advertisers' Service Division (ASD) had a full color flyer of all the Straight Arrow merchandise items available. According to *Sponsor* the Straight Arrow radio show, in less than a year, had earned top-rating as a juvenile show, with a Nielsen rating of 7.5, and had broken into the Nielsen's Top Ten national listings at number eight, the first time a juvenile show had achieved such a distinction.

# Sources

For CDs of all Straight Arrow radio shows available contact Terry Salomonson at:
**Audio Classics Archive**
P O Box 347
Howell, MI 48844-0347
(517) 545-7577
www.audio-classics.com

Howard Culver has a minor "major" role in Jack Webb's *-30-*. VHS copies can be attained from:
**Sheryl Aumack**
7438 West 85th Street
Westchester, CA 90045-2312
(310) 641-5947

(Fred) Howard Wright can be seen in Audie Murphy's *To Hell and Back* (1955) as Mr. Ben Houston and in *The Glass Web* (1953) as Weaver, a receptionist. Both roles are unaccredited.

Gwen Delano can be seen in TV's Dragnet show, "The Big Grandma" which can be purchased from: http://www.shokus.com/crime.html

Back issues of the Straight Arrow *Pow-Wow* and audio cassettes (with a special cassette "jacket") are available from Pow-Wow, c/o Harpers, 301 E. Buena Vista Avenue, North Augusta, SC 29841. For availability and prices send an S.A.S.E. to the above address.

Comments, updates, etc can be sent to the above address or to email address: whhsa@hotmail.com

*Pow-Wow* Newsletter is archived at Michigan State University, Russel B. Nye Popular Culture Collections, Comic Art, East Lansing, MI.

Information on NABISCO Shredded Wheat collectables (including Straight Arrow) can be found at Jean Walton's web site: http://members.aol.com/_ht_a/jwalton971/

### Other informative web sites of OTR interest

http://www.radiogoldindex.com/

http://bearmanormedia.bizland.com/index.html

http://www.oldradio.net/

http://otrsite.com/articles/artjf003.html

http://otrsite.com/

http://www.sperdvac.org

### For Teresa Brewer fans:
http://www.teresafans.org/h.html

### For Jessica Dragonette fans:
http://www.kingtet.com/jessicadragonette/

# Addendum

**HOWARD CULVER'S SCRIPT**

When the Straight Arrow scripts were distributed to the gathered players for a run through Howard Culver would dutifully mark his with his last name or full name or a capital "C." Several cover sheets have artistic renderings of his name with an arrow motif. Other scripts were used as a note pad for doodling or to list things to do, places to go, things to buy and people to meet. There were mathematical figuring, telephone numbers and simple doodling with numbers. Howard dabbled with art. One script had several drawings of a stop watch, glasses, and a Straight Arrow script. He also drew colorful geometrical groupings using green, blue and red pencils. There is even a unusual nude drawing with effective use of shading. Such notes as "Parley/St. Joseph Hosp./Burbank/Wed 15" were straight forward, but there were cryptic messages such as one that read in a list "Shave/Office/Bank/Tie/Morgans." To assist himself in keeping his dual roles separate Culver used blue pencil to circle "Steve" and red for "Straight Arrow".

**BINGMAN'S DRAWINGS**

Another "hand and mind" attempt to quell the need to smoke was Bingman's drawings. He had drawn cartoons and doodles while in high school. He would often draw a cartoon depicting literal translation of a scene from a Straight Arrow script. These became quite popular and were displayed for all to enjoy.

**ORIGIN OF STRAIGHT ARROW?**

At the time we were preparing to launch the Straight Arrow *Pow-Wow* newsletter we thought that we had located the concept of the Straight

Arrow character in the pages of Laura Lee Hope's book, *The Bobbsey Twins on a Houseboat*. The novel, originally published in 1915, has a 1955 reprint date. In the book was a story of an Indian tribe whose totem disappeared at the same time their future chief eloped! Years later, when the son of this love story returned to his parent's tribe, he was questioned as to the whereabouts of the missing totem. The returning Indian's name was "Straight Arrow" and the missing totem was a golden arrow! Unfortunately further research revealed that when the book's copyright was renewed in 1955, the contents were totally rewritten and it was then that the Straight Arrow story was added. It is still curious to think that whoever wrote the revised edition included an obvious copy of the Straight Arrow story.

### INDIANS AND FIRE WATER

Sidney Silleck, Jr., substantiated a story that Sheldon Stark liked to tell about his membership in the Iroquois Federation. Silleck said that Stu Boyd, advertising manager of Nabisco during the Straight Arrow days, and others were invited to Niagara Falls to receive special recognition for their involvement with the Straight Arrow radio production. Boyd in turn invited Federation Indian Chiefs to his room for a drink. Canadian Royal Mounties appeared and arrested Boyd because, at the time, it was against the law to give Indians "firewater."

### STEVE ADAMS/STRAIGHT ARROW "ORIGINS"

The opening dialogue of every Straight Arrow radio show linked Steve Adams and Straight Arrow together as one and the same. However, the actual wording led many to the conclusion that Straight Arrow was really a white man disguised as an Indian. Sheldon Stark, scripter of all the radio shows, could not recall an "origin" story on radio, but he did write a "Story of Straight Arrow" that was condensed and printed on the inside back cover of the 1951 premium, the Injun-Uity Manual. The story told of Steve Adams rescuing Packy from five "bad hats" and escaping by hiding in an abandoned shack which hid the "Cave of Gold." The wounded Packy and a desperate Adams were led to safety by a golden palomino. In the cave with Comanche garb, etc, Packy, who had been thinking about the legend of a "Straight Arrow" heard round the Comanche camp fires, learned that Adams was an Indian raised on the Broken Bow Ranch by the Adamses, who had since died and left the ranch to Adams as well as giving him the name "Steve Adams." The necklace around Adams's neck identified him as the "Straight Arrow"! Afterwards Straight Arrow rode from the Cave of Gold for the first time. This mystical story left more questions than answers about the "origin" of Straight Arrow.

The Magazine Enterprise (ME) Straight Arrow comics introduced in 1949/1950 read similar to the radio scripts. Gardner Fox, who remarked that he had written all the comic stories and daily strips, penned stories that had Packy McCloud teaching the infant Straight Arrow the ways of the white men. The opening strip has Packy as the one "who found the infant Comanche and raised him to manhood, concealing his origin - even from such a tried and true friend as Mesquite Molly." However, in the comics, Mesquite is given credit to helping raise up the young Steve Adams! In ME Straight Arrow #20 (1951) Straight Arrow thinks Packy is dead and sadly remembers how the Packy taught him to read and write and "all that I know! I was just a wild Indian kid…How wise I thought you were. How brave!…" In issue #27 (1952) and # 33 (1953) Straight Arrow is again depicted as an Indian youth growing up in an Indian camp. Neither the comics nor the daily strips (nor for that matter the radio show) gave much background on how Straight Arrow became Steve Adams or vice versa.

## STRAIGHT ARROW PORN

It is hard to imagine that Straight Arrow, who was always on the trail of justice, would ever be considered elsewise, but our hero was the subject of a tract commonly refeered to as a "Tijuana Bible." These booklets were pornographic tracts typically consisting of a cover and eight stapled comic-strip frames portraying characters and celebrities engaged in lewd sexual acts. Most of the art work was extremely crude. The name "straight arrow," aside from it meanings "a morally upright person," has sexual connotations which leant itself to this type of portrayal. These books were available from the early 1900s until sometime in the 1950s. Currently there is a book as well as several web-sites dedicated to these titillating books.

## HOW TALL WAS STRAIGHT ARROW?

At the February 9, 1980 monthly meeting of SPERDVAC (Society to Preserve and Encourage Radio Drama Variety And Comedy) Howard Culver as guest speaker reflected on his years in radio. He alluded to the magic of radio that allows a short person to be "seen" as a tall heroic figure. To demonstrated this he told of an incident that happen to him in 1949. After a Thursday Straight Arrow show he headed for Los Vegas. Cruising along on a near deserted highway "heavy on the accelerator" as Howard recalled he was pulled over by the California Highway Patrol.

"'Going pretty fast? Weren't you'

'Don't know? How fast was I going?'

'About 85!'

'Sorry I did not realize I was going that fast!'

So I gave him my driver license. He looks at it, 'Howard Culver, Hollywood, Actor—What do you do?'

'Radio mostly'

'Oh, radio! Do you do any shows I might hear?'

'Well I am doing one you might have heard if you got a kid'

'I got kids. What show is it'

'Straight Arrow!'

'No kidding?'

Now here is a 6 foot 3 inch CHP officer and he is looking down at a 5 foot 8 inch and he said 'What do you do on Straight Arrow?'

'Straight Arrow'

'Ohhh!!!'

I said, 'I play both Steve Adam and Straight Arrow'

'Well—If you play Straight Arrow give me the Indian war cry'

So out in the middle of the California desserts, not a soul with in 50 miles, except coyotes, Gila monsters, lizards—I cut loose with the biggest, KANEEWAH, FURY! And as I did his eyes got the size of a saucer. And he said 'My God you are Straight Arrow!' He handed me back my driver license and said 'Go on your way. If I went home and told my kids I'd given Straight Arrow a ticket they wouldn't let me in the house!'"

This is just an indication of what the visual image radio created.

**NOTE:** The above is used by permission of SPERDVAC, Society to Preserve and Encourage Radio Drama Variety And Comedy. Join today! At the website you can get started by ordering a membership kit: http://www.sperdvac.org, If you are within the 310 area code call 219-0053 if not in area code 310 call toll free 1-877-251-5771 or write SPERDVAC, P O Box 7177, Van Nuys CA 91409-7177.

## WHAT WOULD YOU HAVE NAMED STRAIGHT ARROW'S HORSE?

Straight Arrow fans are so use to hearing the familiar ejaculation; "Kawneewah, Fury!" that it is nearly impossible to fill-in another name for "Fury" and yet Straight Arrow rode for eleven shows on a nameless palomino. Ralene (later her mother changed the name spelling to Raylene, as she was being called Rawlene) Conner of Huntington Park, California selected three names, from a list of forty-three she created, which she submitted along with a Nabisco Shredded Wheat box-top in hopes to win the prize of a palomino colt and tack or a $1,000. The three names Raylene thought would make suitable names were; Spotted Eagle, Silver Cloud and Running Wind. Nearly fifty-nine years later Raylene wrote, "no wonder I did not win!" Raylene did receive three two-red feathered headbands for her efforts. What would you have named the great golden palomino?

# A Word About the Author

William Harper, currently living in North Augusta, South Carolina, was born 1941 in Teresa Brewer's hometown of Toledo, Ohio. He has had many career opportunities in his life from milk man, candy man warehouse worker, produce clerk at the A&P, loan closer and collector, newspaper "fly catcher", P&G repacker, public and private school teacher, news papering (printing, graphic design, news gathering, ad selling), and now semi retired working part-time as Pastoral Assistant at The Church of the Most Holy Trinity in Augusta, Georgia.

He caught the tail end of the so called "Golden Age" of everything—especially radio and comics! Through out his life the Straight Arrow Nabisco Shredded Wheat jingle has stayed with him as well as the Teddy Bear's Picnic (theme song for Big John and Sparkie), Tom Stetson and the Giant Jungle Ants, the theme song for Hippity Hop (that's another story) and his love and devotion to Saint Joan of Arc. Finding a small cache of Straight Arrow comics started him and his family down the sprawling road of research, spawning the newsletter, *Pow-Wow*.

He and his wife, Teresa (1953-1997), worked together as a team producing prize winning ad designs and articles for the local newspaper, *The Star*, art directors of *The Spectator Magazine* and editors/publishers of *Pow-Wow* and *FCA & ME, Too!*, a fanzine for Fawcett and Magazine Enterprises comic book collectors. William was never on-the-air—except for a brief moment on the Don McNeill's Breakfast Club in the summer of 1951.

# BearManorMedia
P O Box 71426 * Albany, GA 31706

## Plain Beautiful:
### The Life of Peggy Ann Garner

The life story of one of Hollywood's most beloved child actors, whose performance in *A Tree Grows in Brooklyn* won her the Oscar.

$19.95            ISBN 1-59393-017-8

## Spotlights & Shadows
### The Albert Salmi Story

You know the face. You know the credit list: *Lost in Space, Escape from the Planet of the Apes, Gunsmoke, Bonanza, Kung Fu, The Twilight Zone* and hundreds more...But who was Albert Salmi?

Sandra Grabman's biography is a frank and loving tribute, combined with many memories from Salmi's family, friends, and co-stars, and includes never-before-published memoirs from the man himself. From humble beginnings—to a highly successful acting career—to a tragic death that shocked the world—Albert Salmi's story is unlike any other you'll ever read.

$19.95            ISBN: 1-59393-001-1

visit www.bearmanormedia.com
Visa & Mastercard accepted. Add $2.50 postage per book.

# CHECK THESE TITLES!
## BearManorMedia.com
### PO Box 71426 • Albany, GA 31708

**Spike Jones Off the Record: The Man Who Murdered Music** by Jordan R. Young
20th anniversary edition, newly revised & updated!
$29.95     ISBN 1-59393-012-7

**Let's Pretend and the Golden Age of Radio** by Arthur Anderson
Revised and expanded, now including a complete log of the show by radio historians Martin Grams, Jr. and Derek Teague!
$19.95     ISBN 1-59393-019-4

**It's That Time Again Vol. 2 – More New Stories of Old-Time Radio.** Edited by Jim Harmon
New adventures of Red Ryder, Baby Snooks, House of Mystery, The Whistler, Jack Benny and more!
$15.00     ISBN 1-59393-006-2

**The Bickersons: A Biography of Radio's Wittiest Program** by Ben Ohmart
Lavishly illustrated, with a foreword by Blanche herself, Frances Langford. A complete history of the program. Biographies of the cast. Scripts. The infamous *Honeymooners*/Jackie Gleason court case. Unused material. And much more!
$19.95     ISBN 1-59393-008-9

**Private Eyelashes: Radio's Lady Detectives** by Jack French
*Phyl Coe Mysteries, The Affairs of Ann Scotland, Defense Attorney, The Adventures of the Thin Man, Front Page Farrell*...radio was just full of babes that knew how to handle themselves. Get the lowdown on every honey who helped grind a heel into crime.
$18.95     ISBN: 0-9714570-8-5

**A Funny Thing Happened On The Way To the Honeymooners...I Had a Life** by Jane Kean
Jane Kean tells all—and tells it like it was. Jane Kean, star of Broadway, films and television, has had a career that has spanned 60 years. Jane is perhaps best known as Trixie in the award-winning television series, *The Honeymooners*.
$17.95     ISBN 0-9714570-9-3

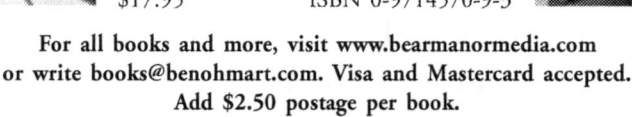

For all books and more, visit www.bearmanormedia.com or write books@benohmart.com. Visa and Mastercard accepted.
Add $2.50 postage per book.

# BearManor Media
## PO Box 71426 • Albany, GA 31708

*Coming in September...*

**HOLD THAT JOAN**
BY BEN OHMART
Finally, a biography of one of the funniest, most overlooked comediennes of the 20th century. The star of television's *I Married Joan* and the film classics *Hold That Ghost*, *Show Business*, *Thin Ice* and many more, very little has been documented about Joan's comical career — until now.
ISBN 1-59393-046-1
$24.95 + $3 US P&H

FOR ALL THESE BOOKS AND MORE VISIT
BEARMANORMEDIA.COM

**THE FIRESIGN THEATRE**
BY FREDERICK C. WIEBEL, JR.
The only book you'll Ever need about the past/present/future masters of American satire. The utterly futile yet complete history of The Firesign Theatre and its also complete recording history is bundled together in one too-large book!
ISBN: 1-59393-043-7. $29.95 + $3 US P&H

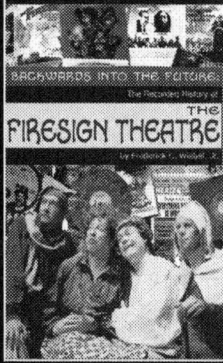

**TALKING TO THE PIANO PLAYER**
BY STUART ODERMAN
Interviews with Marlene Dietrich, Frank Capra, Colleen Moore, Jackie Coogan, Madge Bellamy, Aileen Pringle, Allan Dwan, Adela Rogers St. Johns, Douglas Fairbanks, Jr., and more!
ISBN: 1-59393-013-5
$19.95 + $3 US P&H

**NAMES YOU NEVER REMEMBER, WITH FACES YOU NEVER FORGET**
BY JUSTIN HUMPHREYS
Illustrated with over 100 photographs, Names interviews the unsung character men who often outshone the stars that surrounded them.
ISBN 1-59393-041-0
$19.95 + $3 US P&H

*Presenting the best in nostalgia and entertainment books...*

## www.BearManorMedia.com

www.ingramcontent.com/pod-product-compliance
Lightning Source LLC
Chambersburg PA
CBHW051929160426
43198CB00012B/2085